SharePoint Onli
Modern Experience
Practical Guide

by
Bijaya Kumar Sahoo

FIRST EDITION 2019

Copyright © BPB Publications, India

ISBN: 978-93-88511-575

Distributors:

BPB PUBLICATIONS
20, Ansari Road, Darya Ganj
New Delhi-110002
Ph: 23254990/23254991

DECCAN AGENCIES
4-3-329, Bank Street,
Hyderabad-500195
Ph: 24756967/24756400

MICRO MEDIA
Shop No. 5, Mahendra Chambers,
150 DN Rd. Next to Capital Cinema,
V.T. (C.S.T.) Station, MUMBAI-400 001
Ph: 22078296/22078297

BPB BOOK CENTRE
376 Old Lajpat Rai Market,
Delhi-110006
Ph: 23861747

Published by Manish Jain for BPB Publications, 20 Ansari Road, Darya Ganj, New Delhi-110002 and Printed by him at Repro India Ltd, Mumbai

About the Author

Bijaya is a Microsoft MVP (Office Servers & Services), having more than 11 years of experience in Microsoft Technologies and specializing in SharePoint. He is the Co-founder of TSInfo Technologies, a SharePoint consulting, training & development company in Bangalore, India. He has been a technology writer for many years and writes many SharePoint articles on his websites SharePointSky.com and EnjoySharePoint.com. Bijaya is a passionate individual who loves public speaking, blogging and training others to use Microsoft products. Before co-founding TSInfo Technologies, he was working with small and large organizations in various SharePoint On-premises as well as SharePoint Online office 365 & various related technologies. Bijaya also likes to publish SharePoint videos on his EnjoySharePoint YouTube Channel.

Reviewers

Sathish Nadarajan is the co-founder of SharePointPals, a community blog site where we can find numerous tips and tricks about SharePoint.

His expertise in Sharepoint includes, SharePoint strategy and roadmap definition, business and technical requirements identification, governance, platform architecture, solution design, configuration, development, quality assurance, training, postproduction support, team lead and overall project delivery.

Sathish has been awarded as Most Valuable Professional (MVP) from Microsoft for Office Servers and Services.

Sathish holds a Masters in Technology (M.Tech) as well as Business Administration. Reach out to Sathish by writing at nadarajan.sathish@gmail.com

Bhawana Rathore has received the most prestigious award by Microsoft as an MVP in the year 2018 for Office Apps and Services. Also, she is a passionate SharePoint Architect having around 10 years of IT experience in the industry, In the past, she has worked for IBM, Genisys, TCS as a SharePoint Consultant. Being a SharePoint consultant she has worked on various versions of SharePoint like SharePoint Online, Office 365, SharePoint (2019, 2016,2013,2010). Other technologies she has worked on are ASP.Net, C#, PowerBI, Web Designing. She has written many technical Blogs/Articles which can be read at https://www.enjoysharepoint.com/, https://www.sharepointsky.com/. Video tutorials in SharePoint are also available by her on https://www.youtube.com/enjoysharepoint.

Preface

Greetings all my readers! I am Bijaya Kumar Sahoo, co-founder of TSInfo Technologies and the author of SharePoint Online modern experience practical guide. I will share the idea of why I decided to write this book on SharePoint modern experience.

Let me first introduce a little bit about myself. After working for 11+ years in IT, I have decided to start my own SharePoint consulting company. SharePoint is what we do in our startup and apart from consulting we do provide SharePoint development & training. I do my best to give customer satisfaction in all the areas I am working in my current role.

As you might know, lots of organizations already started using SharePoint modern experience and also you might have come across scenarios where your organization is trying to move to modern experience from SharePoint classic experience.

So I thought of writing this book where you can learn how we can use SharePoint modern experience, how to use different modern web parts and finally, you can learn how to design various portals or pages in SharePoint Online modern sites.

Also, Microsoft has already introduced very powerful data services like Microsoft PowerApps, Flow, PowerBI, etc. which you can use in SharePoint modern sites.

While working with SharePoint classic site I realize we can do lots of beautiful site by using some code which may require little development effort also. But when started using SharePoint modern experience, I saw without using any code, we can build very interactive, responsive and attractive pages very easily. That's when I got the idea of writing a book which will have almost all the web parts, how effectively we can use those web parts in creating attractive pages.

I am sure this book will help you to learn how you can start with SharePoint modern experience, how can you use various web parts to design various pages in modern SharePoint sites.

Not only in SharePoint Online, but you can also learn how to work with modern experience in SharePoint server 2019, the latest version of SharePoint on-premises that Microsoft released.

Acknowledgements

Writing the book was difficult than what I thought at the beginning, let me accept this, but it feels more rewarding as well.

First of all, thanks to everyone associated with this book journey including Manaal, BPB publications and team for the opportunity to publish this book.

This book would not have been possible without the support and encouragement from my dearest friend Bhawana Rathore. I thank her for her faith and confidence in me to take a step forward and become an author of a book.

I am also grateful to all of those with whom I have had the pleasure to work during my professional journey. Due to which I learned a lot of things.

I would like to thank my parents and family members who always supported me and agreed with my decisions.

My sincere thanks to Preeti Sahu, who helped me behind the scenes during the book writing journey.

I would like to dedicate this book to my little sister "Nini" who left us at the age of 10 and is watching us from the heaven.

Errata

We take immense pride in our work at BPB Publications and follow best practices to ensure the accuracy of our content to provide with an indulging reading experience to our subscribers. Our readers are our mirrors, and we use their inputs to reflect and improve upon human errors if any, occurred during the publishing processes involved. To let us maintain the quality and help us reach out to any readers who might be having difficulties due to any unforeseen errors, please write to us at :

errata@bpbonline.com

Your support, suggestions and feedbacks are highly appreciated by the BPB Publications' Family.

Table of Contents

1. **Introducing Office 365 and SharePoint Online** 1

   An overview of Office 365 2

      Pay for what you use 3

      Available from one person company to large companies 3

      Almost zero downtime (reliable) 3

      Access from anywhere with any device 3

      Responsive across in any device 4

      Active Directory integration 4

      Take advantages of SharePoint Online 4

      Your data is secure with Office 365 4

      Microsoft provides a few more document management features 4

      Always up to date 5

   Sign up for an Office 365 subscription 5

   SharePoint Online 7

   How an organization can benefit by using SharePoint Online 8

   Summary 8

2. **SharePoint Classic and Modern Experience** 9

   A Classic SharePoint Online Experience 9

   What are Hub Sites in SharePoint Online? 12

      Advantages/Features of a Hub site in SharePoint Online 12

   Introduction to a Modern SharePoint Online Experience 13

   Supported Browsers for Modern Experience in SharePoint Online 13

   The Lifespan of a Classic SharePoint Online Experience 14

   Enable the Modern Experience at the Tenant Level in Office 365 16

      SharePoint Online List or Document Library Switch to New Experience 18

   An Alternate Way to Switch to the Modern UI Experience 19

   Summary 21

3. **Explore Modern SharePoint Online Site – Team Site** 23

   What are Modern SharePoint Online Team Sites? 23

   Add a Modern Team Site from Outlook 24

Create Modern Team Sites from SharePoint Online Modern Admin Center............ 27

Create a SharePoint Online Modern Team Site from the SharePoint
Online Admin Center 30

Create a Classic Team Site in the Classic Admin Center 35

Home Page Look Changes in a Classic Team Site... 38

What is Site Information in SharePoint Online?.. 40

Change the Site Logo in the SharePoint Online Modern Team Site 43

SharePoint Online Modern Site's Site Contents Page.. 46

SharePoint Online Modern Team Site's Site Setting Options 48

Remove the Left Navigation in Modern SharePoint 50

Delete a Modern Team Site 52

Summary 54

4. SharePoint Online Modern Lists 55

What is a Modern SharePoint Online List? 55

How to Create a Modern SharePoint Online List?... 56

  Using the Site contents Option 57

  Using the Add an app Option 59

The Modern SharePoint Online List features 61

  No Ribbon is Available in the Modern SharePoint Online List 61

  Access List Settings Page in the Modern SharePoint Online List 62

  Add a Column in a Modern SharePoint Online List 62

  Add a column in Your Desired Place by Using the + Symbol 66

  List Details Pane 66

  Change the Column Width Easily... 68

  Drag and Drop Any Column to Any Position... 69

  Create an Item in a Modern SharePoint Online List 71

Edit the List Item in the Modern SharePoint Online List... 72

Export to Excel (Browser Other than Internet Explorer).. 74

Create Microsoft Flow 75

PowerApps 76

  Set Up Alerts in the SharePoint Online modern list Using the Alert me Feature 77

Share an Item in the Modern SharePoint Online List.. 78

  Copy Link and Outlook features in the Modern SharePoint List 80

  Stop sharing in the Modern SharePoint Online List Item.. 82

*Order the List column (date column) as Older to Newer and it's Vice Versa
in the Modern SharePoint List* 84

Older to Newer... 84

Newer to Older... 85

Filter by the Column.. 86

Mandatory Field Validation Notification 88

*Easily View Items without any Next Previous buttons in the SharePoint
Online Modern List* 92

Save View in the Modern SharePoint List 92

Group by in one click in the SharePoint Online Modern List 94

Open ECB Menu Just on a Right Click 95

Items that need attention 96

Display user details on mouse hover.. 98

Summary 100

5. Explore SharePoint Online Modern Document Libraries **101**

How to Create a Modern SharePoint Online Document Library? 102

Using the Site contents option 102

Using the Add an app option 104

SharePoint Online Modern Document Library Features 107

Quickly access the library settings page.. 107

Easily create a column in the modern SharePoint document library.......................... 108

Change the column width...111

Easily upload a document in the modern SharePoint Online library..........................111

Easily quick edit bulk data 112

Document Details Pane...113

Tiles View of Documents 115

Compact list..116

Select Documents and Download in a .zip Format...117

Share the Documents with Others 117

Copy Link and Outlook Options 118

Stop Document Sharing 120

Move to Selected Documents from One Site to Another Site 122

Copy to Selected Documents from One Site to Another Site...................................... 125

Select and Bulk Edit properties 126

Create Microsoft Flow 127

Pin to Top of Each Document 128

Export to Excel 129

Alert Me Notification 129

Order the Library Column as Ascending or Descending 130

Mandatory Field Validation Notification 130

Filter by Column 134

Group by the Column 135

Save View as in the Modern SharePoint Document Library 136

Edit View Columns 138

Open the ECB Menu just on a right click 140

Files That Need Attention 141

Edit New Menu 142

Move up and Move down Options of the Edit New Menu 144

Add Templates 147

SharePoint Online Modern List and Library Column
Customization / Formatting Using JSON.. 149

Formatting an Item When a Date Column is Before or After Today's Date 150

Add an Action Button to a Field for Sending an Email 152

Create a Button to Launch a Flow 155

Format a Number Column as a Data Bar 159

Create Clickable Actions Which Turn Field Values into Hyperlinks 161

Quickly How to Change the Background and Text Color of a Column 164

Conditional Formatting Based on the Value in a Text or Choice Field 166

Summary 169

6. SharePoint Online Modern Site Pages **171**

Creating Modern SharePoint Site Pages.. 172

Create a Site page Using Site contents.. 172

Using the Left Navigation Bar 174

What is a SharePoint Online Modern Site Page?....................................... 175

Designing of a Site Page... 175

The Modern SharePoint Online Site Pages Tabs 177

Set a Custom Site Page as a Home Page.. 178

Add a Custom Site Page to the Navigation 179

New Modern SharePoint Online Site Page's Section Layout 180

Properties of the New Section Layout 184

Add Web Parts to a SharePoint Online Modern Site Page 185
    What are Modern SharePoint Web Parts? 185
Summary 188

7. **Explorer SharePoint Online Modern Experience Web Parts** 189
Text 189
    Move and delete Text web part 192
Image 192
File viewer 193
Link 195
Embed 196
Highlighted content 197
Bing maps 198
    Properties 199
Divider 200
Document library (preview) 201
Events 202
GitHub 205
Hero 208
Image gallery 213
JIRA 218
List (preview) 219
News 220
Properties 222
Microsoft Forms 224
    Properties 227
    Preview 227
    Theme 228
    Share 229
    … (More) 230
Office 365 videos 232
People 234
Power BI 239
Quick Chart 240
Quick Links 243

Site activity...248

    Properties...*250*

Sites..250

Properties..252

Twitter (preview) 253

    Properties...*254*

Weather..258

    Properties...*258*

Yammer 259

Timer..262

Markdown 264

Summary 269

8. SharePoint Online Modern Site Design Examples..**271**

Portal 1 – TSInfo New — a software development portal company portal 271

Portal 2 – TSInfo New Home Page...274

Portal 3 – TSInfo Technologies 276

Portal 4 – About TSInfoTechnologies...278

Portal 5 – Training and Development Site..280

Portal 6 – the Project Management page 282

Portal 7 – the New Insurance page..284

Portal 8 – the New TS Corporate portal 286

Summary 288

9. SharePoint 2019 Modern Experience...**289**

A few new features in SharePoint Server 2019 290

Web Application in SharePoint 2019 291

    Create a web application in SharePoint 2019...*292*

    Creating an application using SharePoint 2019 central administration......................*292*

    Creating an application using Microsoft PowerShell *294*

    View all the web applications *295*

Create a site collection in SharePoint Online 296

Modern SharePoint Online team site versus SharePoint 2019 team site 298

    The modern SharePoint Online team site home page.......................................*298*

    The SharePoint 2019 team site home page *299*

Difference between the SharePoint 2019 site and modern SharePoint Online site features 300

Difference between SharePoint 2019 team site lists and SharePoint Online team site lists 303

Difference between the SharePoint 2019 team site library and the SharePoint Online team site library 303

Web parts available in the SharePoint 2019 team site.................................... 304

Web parts not available in the SharePoint 2019 team site............................ 305

    SharePoint 2019 Modern UI 306

Summary 308

10. SharePoint 2019 Communication Site.. 309

SharePoint 2019 communication sites versus SharePoint Online communication sites 310

    Create a SharePoint 2019 communication site 310

    Create a SharePoint Online communication site 312

Difference between a SharePoint 2019 communication site home page and a SharePoint Online communication site home page 315

    The SharePoint 2019 communication site home page.................................. 315

    The SharePoint Online communication site home page.............................. 317

Create the header and footer navigation in a SharePoint online communication site... 318

    Footer navigation.. 326

Availability and non-availability between SharePoint 2019 communication sites and modern SharePoint Online communication sites 331

Difference between a SharePoint 2019 communication site list and SharePoint Online communication site list 334

Difference between a SharePoint 2019 communication site library and SharePoint Online communication site library 335

Web Parts available in a SharePoint 2019 Communication Site.................. 335

Web parts not available in SharePoint 2019 communication site 336

Summary 337

11. SharePoint Online Modern Experience – What's not possible? 339

Customizations unsupported in modern team sites 339

Customization is impossible in a modern document library 340

Summary 341

CHAPTER 1

Introducing Office 365 and Share-Point Online

SharePoint is a web-based business collaboration and document management system by Microsoft. Its content management feature allows organizations or users to securely store, share and collaborate with each other. It is one of the award-winning products from Microsoft which helps millions of organizations to improve productivity.

SharePoint is a web based application by Microsoft that enables organizations to work more efficiently by letting users share documents, data, and information. It provides document management and collaboration features which increases the productivity of an organization.

SharePoint is one of the popular portal technologies. A lot of small to large scale organizations are using SharePoint to develop their portals. It is scalable, extensible, and customizable portal solution for various organizations.

It helps you store, share, and manage digital information within your organization in a better way. In no time, you can create team sites to collaborate with each other. By using SharePoint lists and libraries, you can store information, documents, and so on.

You can access SharePoint in the following two ways:

- SharePoint On-Premises
- SharePoint Online (Office 365)

- In the year 2010, Microsoft provided SharePoint as a part of **Office 365** (**Microsoft Cloud Service**). An organization can use SharePoint without installing anything on their premises.

In Office 365, most of the times, Microsoft releases new features and functionalities in SharePoint Online.

Microsoft has the same user interface in SharePoint known as classic experience. Microsoft is trying to modernize SharePoint so that organizations and users can use SharePoint effectively. So, Microsoft has come up with the modern SharePoint experience or the SharePoint modern UI.

In the year 2017, Microsoft introduced new experiences for SharePoint team sites, communication sites, site pages, list and libraries, and so on.

Here, in this *SharePoint Online Modern Experience Practical Guide* book, we will discuss the following topics:

- What is the modern SharePoint experience (modern UI) in SharePoint?

- What are modern team sites and communication sites?

- What are modern lists and libraries?

- How an organization can be helpful by using Modern SharePoint Online?

- How can we use various web parts in modern SharePoint site pages?

- Finally, we will see how we can make various SharePoint Online portals by using modern experience.

An overview of Office 365

Office 365 is the **cloud** solution or services provided by Microsoft. The services are hosted outside your organization in Microsoft datacenters, and Microsoft cloud is fully maintained by Microsoft.

Office 365 was made available for public on June 2011. As the name suggests, Office 365 provides services such as Office (Word, Excel, PowerPoint, OneNote, Outlook, Publisher, and Access) as well as other services like OneDrive for Business, Exchange Online, Skype for Business, SharePoint Online, Yammer, and so on.

Users can access all the above mentioned services (including server maintenance, patching or update activities) in SharePoint Online without having to worry about maintaining anything On-Premises.

There are various benefits of using Office 365 in an organization. Let's discuss some of these in the following sections.

Pay for what you use

The cloud service Office 365 is available on a subscription-based model from Microsoft. Users can opt for monthly or annual subscription. It has plans for different types of use like personal, home, business, and student. User can subscribe according to their requirement and then, they can access the service from anywhere with any device with an internet connection.

Also, by using Microsoft Office 365 business plans, a user can install the latest Office applications in multiple devices such as PCs, Macs, Android tablets, Android phones, iPads, and iPhones.

Another advantage of the office plans, *Office 365 Business Premium* and *Office 365 Enterprise E3*, is that you can work offline without having an internet connection, and the next time when you connect to the internet, all your changes will be synced and will be up to date.

Available from one person company to large companies

Microsoft Office 365 is available from a very small organization (one person's company) to very large scale organization (50,000+ users). So, you should not be worried about how many users Office 365 can support.

All business users can perform their daily activities such as emailing, document and information management, calendar, collaboration with teams, instant messaging services and so on.

Almost zero downtime (reliable)

Microsoft guarantees that the services will be available with 99.9% uptime. You will have almost zero downtime. Microsoft has various data centers all over the world and if one data center is unavailable, you will continue to receive services from other available data centers.

Apart from this, they also provide 24 x 7 phone support for critical issues (on selected plans).

Access from anywhere with any device

You can access Office 365 and all its services from anywhere and with any device. You can access Office 365 from a desktop, laptop, tablet, or phone. You just need an internet connection for it because all the services are installed in the Microsoft data center.

Microsoft services such as Microsoft Office 365 can now be accessed on Android devices. It provides Office for Android, users can easily work with Word documents, Excel documents or PowerPoint documents from the Android devices.

Responsive across in any device

You can open Microsoft SharePoint Office 365 in any responsive devices like a PC, mobile, tablet, browser, etc. You can access and use SharePoint Office 365 from all these types of responsive devices,

Active Directory integration

Active Directory is a database that keeps track of all the user accounts and passwords in your organization. It allows you to store your user accounts and passwords in one protected location, improving your organization's security.

Active Directory is tightly integrated with Office 365. Also, **Single Sign-On** and synchronization with Active Directory are easier in Office 365.

Take advantages of SharePoint Online

Office 365 provides SharePoint features in terms of SharePoint Online. SharePoint Online is a perfect tool for collaboration and document management for your organization. You can create sites in less than a minute for your team to collaborate, maintain documents, and work with lists, announcements, and blogs, and so on. You can take advantages of check in and check out features, and see various versions of documents.

You can share your documents with external users also in SharePoint Online. SharePoint Online is tightly integrated with Office products. You can work with the Word document and then publish to SharePoint Online directly from Word.

Your data is secure with Office 365

This question comes first when you think of moving your application or data to the cloud. Your data is safe in Microsoft cloud. In Office 365, they use five layers of security to keep an organization's data safe. According to Microsoft, *With Office 365, it's your data. You own it. You control it*. Microsoft never uses any of data for advertising and organizations can take their data any time they want. Microsoft continuously monitors the systems for suspicious activities.

Microsoft provides a few more document management features

Here are a few more document management features provided by Microsoft in SharePoint Online Office 365:

- **Data Loss Prevention (DLP)**: This feature allows you to set granular data policies.

- **Data Loss Prevention (DLP)**: This feature allows you to set granular policies that govern your data and define specific actions taken when information is shared.

- **Advanced Threat Protection (ATP)**: This feature proactively protects your organization against incoming threats.

- **Advanced Threat Protection (ATP)**: This feature protects your organization from incoming threats from external sources.

- **Intelligent Protection:** This is a machine learning algorithm that tracks vulnerabilities.

Microsoft tracks vulnerabilities at scale through machine learning and mitigates them.

Always up to date

- One of the benefits to move to Office 365 is that you will always stay up to date and you will get all the features and functionalities of the latest Microsoft Office products. Whenever newer versions come, everything will be available in Office 365.

Sign up for an Office 365 subscription

Office 365 offers the following subscription plans and you can choose any plan depending on your requirements:

- **Office 365 plans**: As Office 365 is subscription based, the cost depends on the features you use. You can subscribe to features which you need for your company or organization. So it is very much cost effective. Users can opt for a monthly or annual subscription. You can also cancel your subscription at any point of time if you are not satisfied. In the yearly plan, there is an option to choose for a yearly subscription, but you can pay on a monthly basis.

- **Office Education plans**: Office 365 has various office apps for education like OneNote, Sway, Office, OneDrive, Skype, Docs.com, and so on. Sign up with your school email address and Internet Explorer.

- **Office Home plans**:

- Office 365 Home ($89.99 per year)

- Office 365 Personal ($69.99 per year)

- Office Home & Student 2016 ($119.99 one-time purchase) *Price may vary.

You can check the price and compare features on the Microsoft Office 365 official site.

All these plans will have Office products installed and also include Office 2016 apps. You can use your PC, smartphone (Windows Phone, Android Phone or iPhone) and tablets (Windows Tablet, Android Tablet and iPod).

- **Office 365 Business plans**: It has various plans for your business like Office 365 business plans:
- Office 365 Business
- Office 365 Business Essentials
- Office 365 Business Premium
- Office 365 ProPlus
- Office 365 Enterprise E1
- Office 365 Enterprise E3
- Office 365 Enterprise E5
- For example, if you opt for **Office 365 Enterprise E3**, then you will have the following features:
- You will always have the latest Office apps (Office 2016).
- You can use Office products in various devices PCs, laptops, Macs, Windows tablets and iPad and Android, tablets, and most mobile devices. The user can access emails (Outlook) anytime anywhere from your desktop or from the web browser. Each user gets 50 GB of primary mailbox and unlimited storage.
- Users can host online meetings with audio, HD video, and web conferencing over the internet and can join the meeting from the smartphone, tablet, or PC.
- The user can use Skype for Business meetings as well as take advantage of Instant Messenger, voice calls, and video calls using Skype for Business.
- By using OneDrive for Business, users can store 1TB document in the cloud and it can be accessed from anywhere and by using any devices.
- By using Yammer, which provides corporate social network feature, organizations can connect with their employees, share information across teams, and so on.

Apart from features mentioned above, there are a lot of other benefits. You can compare the price and features on the Office 365 official site. (https://products. office.com/en-in/business/compare-more-office-365-for-business-plans)

To start a 30-day trial version, you need to have a Microsoft account and then you can sign up for the **Office 365 Enterprise E3** account. Start now to use services such as Mail, Calendar, People, Yammer, OneDrive, Sites, Tasks, Delve, Video, Word, Excel, PowerPoint, OneNote, Sway, etc.

People can sign up (free trial) in Office 365 by using the following two ways:

- **Office 365 Enterprise E3 Account** (https://www.sharepointsky.com/office-365-trial/**)**
- **Office 365 Developer Program** (https://www.sharepointsky.com/office-365-developer-program/**)**

SharePoint Online

SharePoint Online is a cloud-based service from Microsoft which comes as a part of Office 365. It provides enterprise content management features and helps organizations to connect, share and collaborate within the team, with business partners and customers.

By using SharePoint Online, users can access SharePoint sites, share documents and information from anywhere, anytime and from any device such as a laptop, desktop, tablet, and mobile.

Office 365 provides SharePoint feature in terms of SharePoint Online. SharePoint Online is a perfect tool for collaboration and document management for your organization. You can create sites quickly for your team to collaborate, maintain documents, work with lists, announcements, blogs, and so on. Moreover, you can take advantages of check-in and check out features, see various versions of documents, and do much more. You can also share your documents with external users through SharePoint Online. SharePoint Online is tightly integrated with the Office products and you can work with the Word document and then publish to SharePoint Online directly from Word. Apart from these, there are a number of advantages of SharePoint Online, some of which are mentioned here:

- **Microsoft data centers**: Unlike SharePoint On-Premises version, in SharePoint Online, SharePoint resides in the Microsoft data center. So, Microsoft manages the hardware related stuff, patches maintenance, etc. So, organizations can save cost related to IT admin activities.
- **Quick access to updates**: Microsoft is investing heavily in SharePoint Online, so you will get a lot of new features if you are using SharePoint Online. These features may not be available in SharePoint On-Premises versions or may come latest.
- **Highly secured**: In terms of security, Microsoft implements tight security measures and has been awarded many security certifications, so your data is very much secured.

- **Almost zero downtime**: There is a 99.99% of uptime, so the SharePoint Online site will be always up and running.

How an organization can benefit by using SharePoint Online

Organizations can benefit a lot by using SharePoint Online. Here are a few benefits:

- No hardware, software license costs for SharePoint Online: As an organization, you can access SharePoint Online sites anytime, anywhere and from any devices like a laptop, mobile, and tablet. You do not need to take any hardware or software licenses for it. Organizations can save cost in terms of licensing, hardware, administrators and maintenance costs. Microsoft will take care of the maintenance cost rather than your organization. You just need to use SharePoint.

- Share with external users: You can share SharePoint Online with you internal as well as external users, customers, or vendors. External users do not have a licence to your Office 365 subscription, but they can still access SharePoint online sites with a Microsoft account.

- Stay up-to-date with SharePoint Online: Microsoft releases a lot of new features in SharePoint Online regularly. If you are using SharePoint Online, you will get updated features regularly by Microsoft.

Summary

In this chapter, we learned about SharePoint Online and its advantages. The usage of SharePoint Online has spread worldwide in this modern era because of its user-friendly interface that enables you to drag and drop the file you want to save on cloud. Moreover, it keeps your files secured and makes them available for you each time you need them urgently. In the next chapter, we will learn the compatibility, user experience, document library, and modern UI of SharePoint Online.

CHAPTER 2

SharePoint Classic and Modern Experience

Before going further, let us see how SharePoint Online classic and modern sites look like.

In this chapter, we will cover the following topics:

- A classic SharePoint Online experience
- A modern SharePoint Online experience
- Supported browsers for a modern experience in SharePoint Online
- The lifespan of a classic SharePoint Online experience
- Enable the modern experience at the tenant level in Office 365
- The SharePoint Online list or document library switch to a new experience
- An alternate way to switch to the modern UI experience

A Classic SharePoint Online Experience

Here, I will show you how a SharePoint Online classic site looks like:

1. **View of a classic SharePoint home page:** This is the default page which appears when a user opens a SharePoint Online classic site. The following screenshot represents the home page of a classic **SharePoint Team** site (**SharePointSky Team**) where you can see the left navigation contents, promoted links, news feeds and so on.

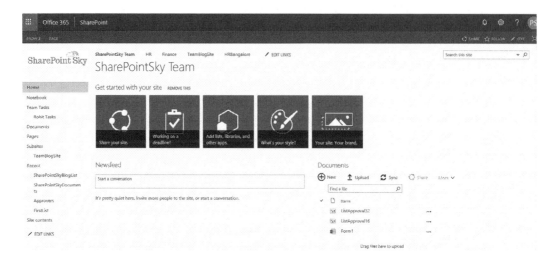

2. **View of a classic SharePoint Online site contents page**: The following is a screenshot of the site contents page of a classic SharePoint Online site. You can view a list of all libraries and lists of the SharePoint site:

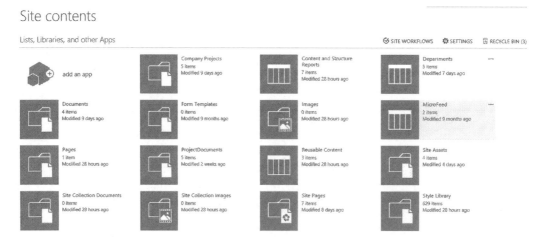

3. **View of a classic SharePoint list**: If you open a list of a classic SharePoint team site, then you will see the classic SharePoint list (**SharePointSky Blog List**) as shown in the following screenshot:

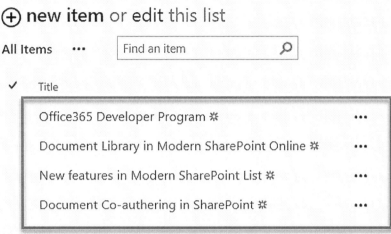

4. **View of a classic SharePoint Online document library**: When you open the document library of a classic SharePoint team site, you will see the classic SharePoint document library (**SharePointSky Documents**) as shown in the following screenshot:

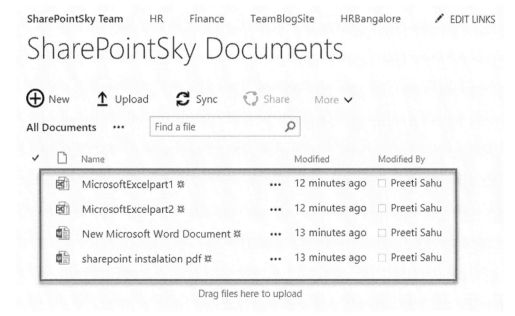

What are Hub Sites in SharePoint Online?

In an organization, a lot of sites grow with time. They can be team sites or newly introduced communication sites. So, it is difficult to manage the number of sites.

A hub site helps bring together team sites and communication sites, provides the capabilities to organize sites in a better way and also increases visibility and navigation among associated sites.

Microsoft announced SharePoint hub sites, new building blocks of the intranet, to bring together related sites to roll up news and activities, to simplify search, and to create cohesion with shared navigation and look and feel. Ultimately giving your business the flexibility and agility to dynamically grow and respond to the changes in business, without rigid silos, and helping bind a more cohesive workforce moving forward in the same direction.

As an organization, you may need to change the site structure and contents within the sites for your business need. Hub sites will give you this flexibility to navigate easily.

Hub sites can be created by a user with the SharePoint Administrator role in Office 365 admin centre or by using PowerShell and site owners can then join a team site or communication site under a hub site.

Advantages/Features of a Hub site in SharePoint Online

Now, we will discuss a few advantages/features of using a hub site in SharePoint Online.

- Hub sites bring your organizations' team sites and communication sites together.

- Hub sites display news, events and site activities across all the sites (both team sites and communication sites). Your users will be able to stay up-to-date with the latest news and events within one location.

- When you search at a hub, you can automatically search from all the related sites. When you search at any sites which are joined, they will have the same search experience as the hub level. In short, the search experience will appear for the hub site as well as for all the team sites and communication sites joined to the hub site. Internally, a search scope is created which allows users to directly search for content within all the joined sites.

- Hub sites display cross-site navigation, which means you will see a top navigation bar on the hub site as well as on all the joined sites (both team sites and communication sites). So, navigation to any site will be easier. Consistent navigation will always be there in any joined site as well as in hub sites.

- When you join a team site or communication site under a hub site, the site inherits the look and feel, theme, and logo from the hub site level. All the joined team sites and communication sites will have the same consistent look and feel.

Introduction to a Modern SharePoint Online Experience

According to Microsoft, modern SharePoint is a whole new user experience. It's more than a fresh look and it's designed from the ground up to work on mobile devices. It is fully responsive.

The modern experiences in SharePoint Online are:

- Modern team sites
- Modern list and library experiences
- Modern site pages
- Modern Communication site

Compared to the SharePoint classic experience, SharePoint Online modern UI has a better and updated user experience, faster page loading, more intuitive, and responsive design. We will discuss the various advantages of modern team sites, list and libraries as well as site pages in detail in the upcoming chapters.

As an organization, you should start using modern SharePoint sites. The new experience will increase the user experience which increases productivity.

Supported Browsers for Modern Experience in SharePoint Online

The following is a list of browsers that support the SharePoint Online modern experience:

- Latest version of Mozilla Firefox
- Latest version of Google Chrome

- Latest version of Safari
- Latest version of Microsoft Edge
- Internet Explorer 10 and 11

The Lifespan of a Classic SharePoint Online Experience

In classic SharePoint sites, organizations do a lot of customization in pages, lists or libraries using script injections (using the Script Editor Web Part or Content Editor Web Part). But this customization is not supported by SharePoint Online modern sites.

You should plan to move things from the classic SharePoint to the modern UI. But one question that comes to my mind is what will be the lifespan of classic SharePoint Online experience? Well, there is a specific date declared by Microsoft but you should start analyzing and try migrating to the new interface. Both classic and modern SharePoint Online experience will coexist:

1. **View of a modern SharePoint home page**: The following screenshot represents the home page of a modern SharePoint team site (**SharePointSky New Team**) where you can see the left navigation, activity, news, quick links and so on:

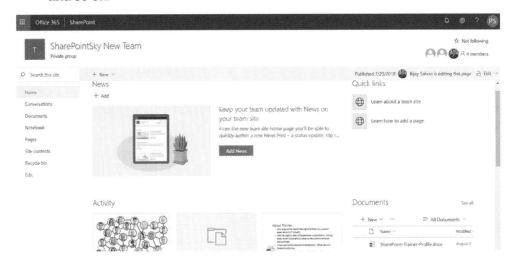

2. **View of a modern SharePoint site list**: If you open a list of the modern SharePoint Online team site, you will see the modern SharePoint Online list (**SharePointSky New Blog List**) as shown in the following screenshot:

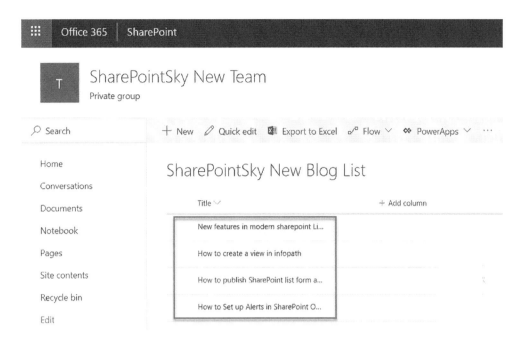

3. **View of a modern SharePoint Online document library**: When you open the document library of the modern SharePoint team site, you will see the modern SharePoint document library (**SharePointSky New Documents**) as shown in the following screenshot:

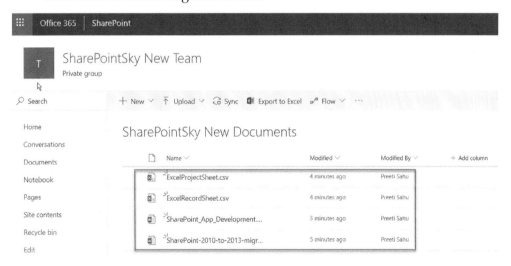

Enable the Modern Experience at the Tenant Level in Office 365

If you are already using the SharePoint classic experience and you would want to use the SharePoint modern experience, then first you need to enable it at the tenant level. Unless you enable the modern experience, administrators will not be able to use the modern UI. They will not even be able to create a modern team site.

If your organization is not ready to use the modern experience in SharePoint, then it is better to disable it at the tenant level at least for the production sites.

If your site has customizations using custom scripts, then you cannot move to the modern experience directly. Similarly, if your organization is still using InfoPath forms, then it might not work properly in modern sites.

We can enable or disable the SharePoint Online modern experience at the tenant level. If you do not want to use the new SharePoint Online experience, then the best way is to disable it at the tenant level. Follow the given steps to enable or disable the SharePoint Online new experience:

2. First, go to **Microsoft 365 admin center** on your existing profile. Then, click on the **SharePoint** option from the **Admin centers** tab as shown in the following screenshot:

2. When you click on the **SharePoint** option, the **SharePoint admin center** page appears on the screen. Then, click on **settings** as shown in the following screenshot:

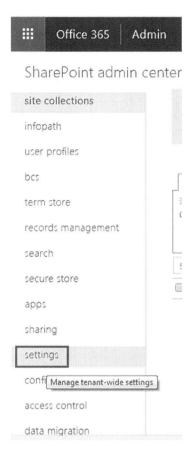

3. On the settings page, you can see the **SharePoint Lists and Libraries experience** tab. If you do not want to use the new experience, then you can click on the **Classic experience** radio button. But if you want to use the new experience, you can click on the **New experience (auto detect)** radio button. Remember even if you select **New experience (auto detect)** at the tenant level, you still have the option to control at the site collection level, site level and even at the list and document library level:

SharePoint Lists and Libraries experience

The new experience gives people improved performance, additional phone and tablet features, and a simplified UI. Select the new experience (auto detect) option when you want to use the classic experience for libraries that have features or customizations enabled that only work in the classic experience, and use the new experience for libraries that don't have these features or customizations enabled. If you select the new experience, users can still switch to the classic experience if they want. Select the classic experience if you're not ready for your users to switch to the new experience.

Classic experience

New experience (auto detect)

SharePoint Online List or Document Library Switch to New Experience

We can also enable or disable the modern experience at the list level or document library level to use the new experience in SharePoint Online. Follow the given steps:

1. Open the **List settings** or **Library settings** page as shown here:

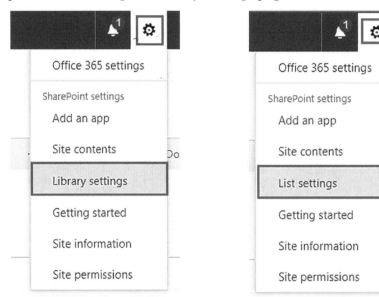

2. On the **List settings** or **Library settings** page, click on the **Advanced settings** hyperlink option under the **General settings** tab. This will open the **Advanced settings** page as shown in the following screenshot:

3. On the **Advance settings** page, click on the **List experience** tab to view the list, and here, you will see the following three options:

    • **Default experience set by my administrator**: This option will take the default experience set by the administrator.

    • **New experience**: Choose this option if you want to use the new experience of the SharePoint Online list or document library. If you choose this option, then every time you open the list or library, you will see the modern UI for the particular list or library.

    • **Classic experience**: Choose this option if you want to use the SharePoint classic experience.

4. Then, click on the **OK** option.

List experience

Select the experience you want to use for this list. The new experience is faster, has more features, and works better across different devices.

Display this list using the new or classic experience?
  ○ Default experience set by my administrator
  ⊙ New experience
  ○ Classic experience

| OK | Cancel |

An Alternate Way to Switch to the Modern UI Experience

If the new experience is enabled at the tenant level, then you can very easily switch to the new modern UI and you can easily switch back to the classic experience in SharePoint Online. You can do changes in your list or document library as well as on your site contents page:

1. Open the SharePoint Online document library, list or site contents page. On the bottom left-hand corner of the page, click on the **Return to classic SharePoint** tab if the library is open in the modern UI or click on the **Exit classic experience** link if you are using the classic UI.

2. In the following screenshot, you can see the **Exit classic experience** link because I am using the classic SharePoint UI. You need to click on the link to switch to the modern UI:

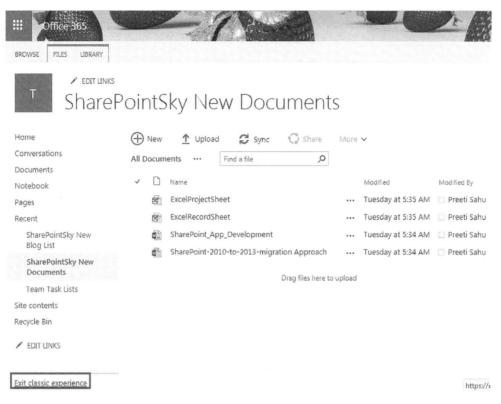

3. When you click on **Exit classic experience**, the SharePoint document library will open which is the **Modern SharePoint Document Library** as shown in the following screenshot:

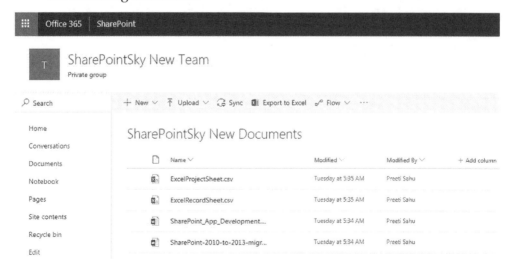

Summary

In this chapter, we saw the classic and modern SharePoint experience. We learned that various browsers support SharePoint Online modern experience. We also learned about the lifespan of a classic SharePoint Online experience, how to enable the modern experience at the tenant level in Office 365 and how to switch to the new list or library experience from SharePoint Online classic experience. We also discussed an alternate way to switch to the modern UI experience.

In the next chapter, we will discuss about modern SharePoint Online team site Office 365, how to create a SharePoint Online modern team site in Office 365, and various ways to customize a SharePoint Online modern team site.

CHAPTER 3

Explore Modern SharePoint Online Site – Team Site

In this chapter, we will discuss about modern SharePoint Online team sites. We will discuss how to create a modern team site from SharePoint Online modern Admin Center and how to customize the SharePoint Online modern team site such as you can change the site logo, title, description, remove left navigation, etc.

What are Modern SharePoint Online Team Sites?

A modern team site in SharePoint Online is more interactive, responsive, loads faster, etc. When you create a modern team site, it automatically creates the O365 group, group email address, and ability to identify whether this site contains sensitive data (privacy).

Modern team sites are integrated with Office 365 groups and provide options to collaborate better than before. Office 365 Groups bring together conversations and calendar from Outlook, files from SharePoint sites, tasks from Planners, etc. into a single collaboration space.

By default, when the modern team site is created, all the users, who are members of the site, will automatically be added to the group.

The home page of a modern team site looks more interactive. It highlights new, site activity and important documents, with quick access to Office 365 Groups, its members and associated Office 365 apps.

Also, modern team sites work seamlessly in mobile apps as well. This way it increases the usability of SharePoint, collaborate on the go!

Add a Modern Team Site from Outlook

You can create a modern SharePoint Online team site from your Outlook. Open your Microsoft Outlook and click on the + symbol of **Groups**.

Once you click on the + symbol, you need to fill all the fields of the group. The fields are as follows:

- **Group name:** You need to provide a name for the Group which you want to create.

- **Group email address:** When you enter the group name, at the same time, the group email address will be automatically generated.

- **Description:** You need to provide some description about the group which you want to create.

- **Privacy:** If you want to keep this group as **Private** or **Public,** then select the option from the dropdown as per your requirement.

- **Language for group-related notifications:** Select a language for the group-related notifications.

When all the fields are completed, click on **Create** as shown in the following screenshot:

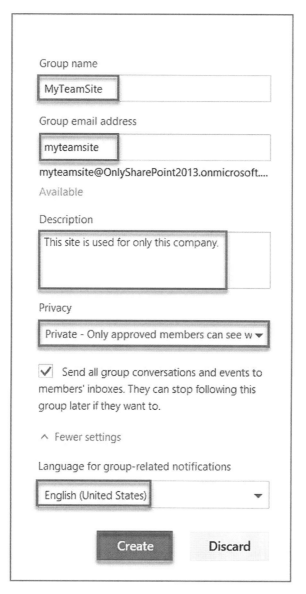

When you click on the **Create** option, it will ask you to add the members you want to add to the group which you have created. Add all members who you want and then click on **Add** as shown in the following screenshot:

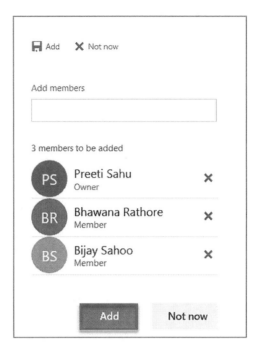

When you add the members, you can see your created team site as shown in the following screenshot:

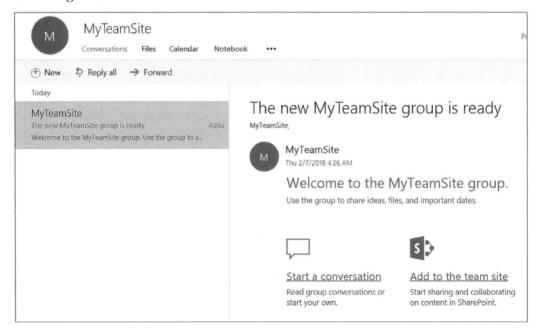

Create Modern Team Sites from SharePoint Online Modern Admin Center

Follow the given steps to create a modern team site:

1. Go to the home page of SharePoint site collection, click on the app launcher icon. Select the **SharePoint** tile and then click on the **+ Create site** tab (if you don't see this option, then your self-service site creation is not enabled for your ID) as shown in the following screenshot:

2. Select the Team site option and enter the name and description in the **Site name** and **Site description** tabs:

Site name

Site description

Tell people the purpose of this site

Next   Cancel

3. While entering the name, it automatically shows the **Group email address** (first picks the site name as the group email address. If it's not available, then you can click on the edit icon to input an alternate address) and then in the **Site description** box, add some text and select the **Privacy settings** as shown in the following screenshot. Once completed, click on **Next**:

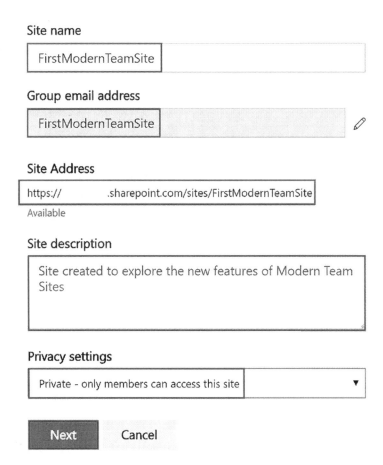

FirstModernTeamSite
Private group

Who do you want to add?
You can also add more people later

Add additional owners

Enter a name or email address

Add members

Enter a name or email address

Members will receive group conversations and events in their inbox. They can unsubscribe at any time by clicking the unsubscribe link in group emails.

Finish

5. Once done, you can see your modern team site as **FirstModernTeamSite** as shown in the following screenshot:

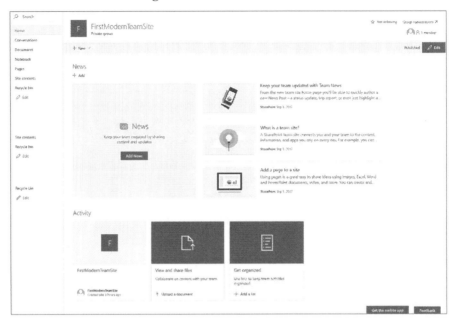

Create a SharePoint Online Modern Team Site from the SharePoint Online Admin Center

An office 365 administrator can easily create a SharePoint Online modern team site from the SharePoint Online admin center.

SharePoint Online admin center URL: https://<tenantname>-admin.sharepoint.com

If you are using the old SharePoint Online admin center, then you will not be able to see the option to create a modern SharePoint Online team site as shown in the following screenshot:

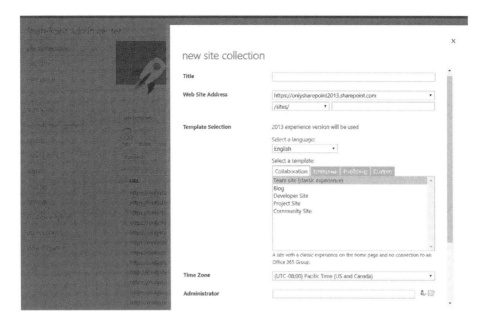

But you can create it from the SharePoint Online new admin center as follows:

1. Go to **SharePoint admin center**, and click on **Try it now** to go to the new SharePoint Online admin center:

2. In the new SharePoint Online admin center, click on **Active Sites** under **Sites** in the left pane.

3. From the ribbon, click on the **+ Create** button as shown in the following screenshot:

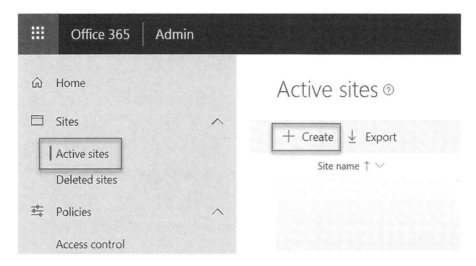

4. In SharePoint Online, it will show you options to create **Team site** or **Communication** site as shown in the following screenshot:

Create a site
Choose the type of site you'd like to create.

Team site
Share documents, have conversations with your team, keep track of events, manage tasks, and more with a site connected to an Office 365 group.

Communication site
Publish dynamic, beautiful content to people in your organization to keep them informed and engaged on topics, events, or projects.

Other options
Create a new team site without an Office 365 group, or a Document center, Enterprise wiki, Publishing portal, or Project Web App site.

5. Click on **Team site**.

6. Then, it will ask you to provide the following details:

   - **Site name**
   - **Group owner**
   - **Select a language**

7. This is shown in the following screenshot:

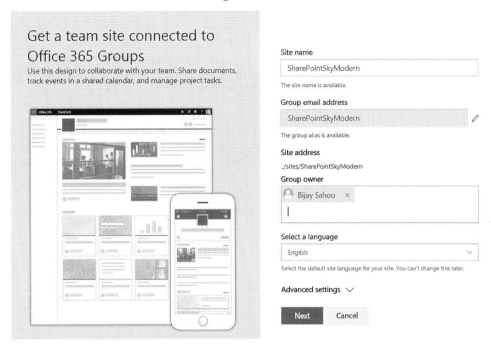

8. You can also expand the **Advanced settings** option and provide information as follows:

- **Privacy settings**: You can choose the settings as private or public. Private sites can be accessible by only members and public sites can be accessible by anyone in the organization.

- **Time zone**: You can select the time zone to a specified time zone.

- **Site description**: You can add some text to provide site description.

- **Storage limit**: You need to enter the amount of storage.

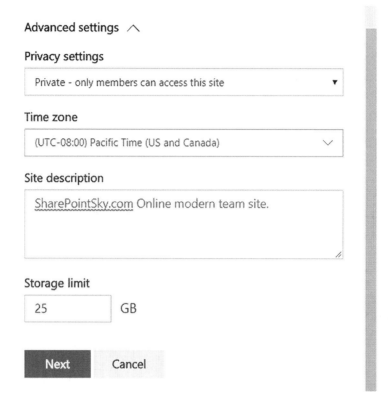

9. Then, click on **Next**. The next page asks you to add additional members. Here, you can add additional owners and members as shown here:

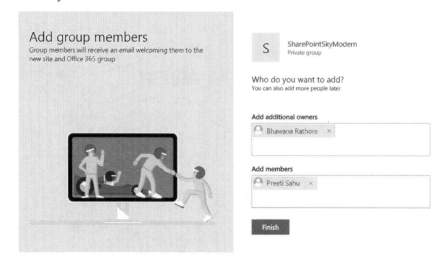

10. Once you click on **Finish,** the site is created as shown in the following screenshot. For example: https://onlysharepoint2013.sharepoint.com/ sites/SharePointSkyModern:

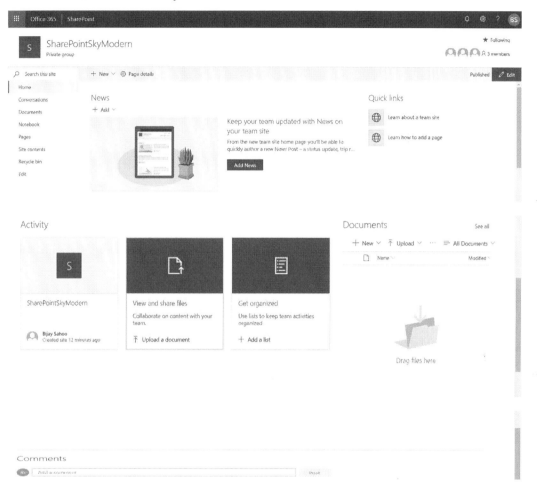

Create a Classic Team Site in the Classic Admin Center

Follow the given steps to create a classic team site:

1. Go to **Office 365 Admin Center** and click on the **SharePoint** option. In **SharePoint Admin Center**, go to the **New** option which is present in the ribbon to create a new SharePoint team site:

2. After clicking on the **New** option, the **new site collection** page opens, where you need to fill the details of the new site for all the fields as follows:

    • **Title**: Enter your site title

    • **Web Site Address**: Enter your web site address

    • **Template Selection**: Select your language and select the template as "Team site classic experience

    • **Time Zone**: Choose your time zone from the drop-down menu

    • **Administrator**: Enter your administrator name through the people picker

    • **Storage Quota**: Give a specific number for the storage limit

    • **Server Resource Quota**: Enter a server resource quota number

3. And then click on **OK** to create a new team site as shown in the following screenshot:

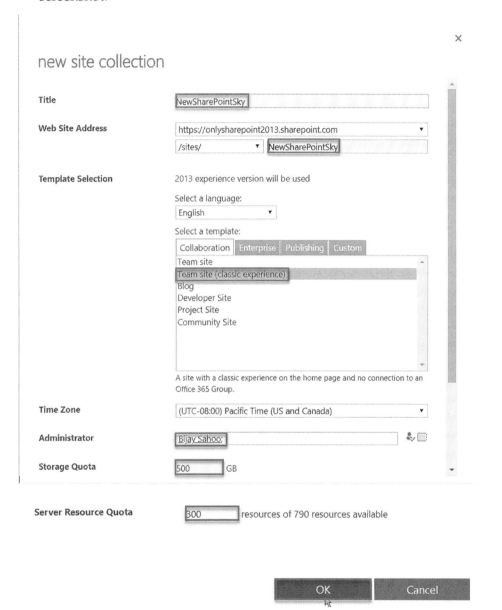

Note (Storage quota): The storage depends on the Office 365 plan you have taken. In Office 365 Enterprise E1, E3, or E5, or SharePoint Online Plan 1 or 2, Microsoft provides 1 TB per organization plus 10 GB per license purchased.

Also Storage for site collections depends on the plan, in the above plan, you can have up to 25 TB per site collection or group.

But any time you can purchase an unlimited amount of additional SharePoint Online storage. Check out an article from Microsoft: https://docs.microsoft.com/en-us/office365/servicedescriptions/sharepoint-online-service-description/sharepoint-online-limits

Note (Server Resource Quota): The resource quota is very much useful if you are using sandbox solutions in your site collection. By using server resource quotas you can limit the risk that sandbox custom code can have on available resources on a site collection.

Suppose you do not want to allow any sandbox solution in your site collection, then you can set it to zero. By default the number is 300.

Remember a bad sandbox solution code can increase your CPU & RAM usage to very high.

Home Page Look Changes in a Classic Team Site

Home page look changes help you to change the colors of your SharePoint Online site. This means it changes the color of your home page in SharePoint Online:

1. To change the color of your home page, go to the gear icon which is located at the top right-hand corner of your profile home page. Then, click on to the **Change the look** option from the drop-down menu:

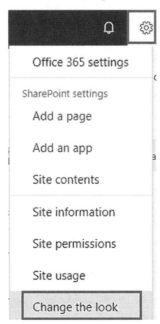

2. After clicking on the **Change the look** option, the **Change the look** page opens where you can see different types of themes. You need to select any one of the themes and just click on the **Apply** option to apply that theme to your home page:

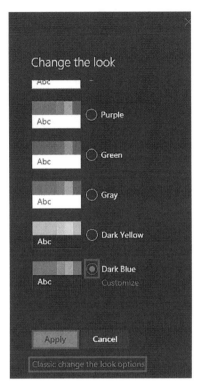

3. If you click on **Classic change the look options**, you will see the page, which has a classic look, as shown in the following screenshot. You can also change the look of the home page in modern SharePoint by using classic themes.

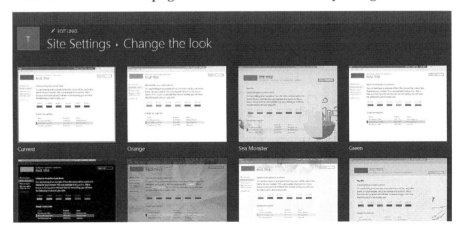

4. Finally, the modern home page will look as shown in the following screenshot:

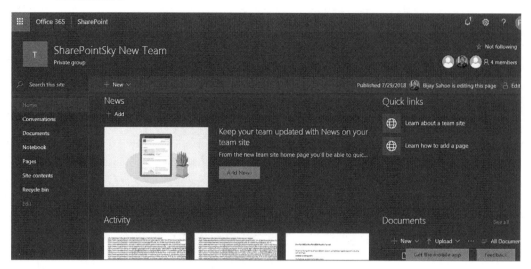

What is Site Information in SharePoint Online?

Site information contains all the information about the SharePoint site in SharePoint Online. In short, the SharePoint site information holds the details of the SharePoint site such as **Site name**, **Site description**, **Privacy settings,** and so on.

If you want to see the details of your site, then follow the given steps:

1. First, go to the Gear icon which is located at the top right-hand corner of your SharePoint profile home page. Then, click on the **Site information** option from the drop-down menu.

2. After clicking on the **Site information** option, the **Edit site information** page appears as shown in the following screenshot.

On this page, you can see the details of your SharePoint site as follows:

3. **Site logo:** If you want to change the **Site logo**, then click on the **Change** option which can be found under the **Site logo** option. Using the **Change** option, you can select your logo from your PC or any browser, etc.

   - **Site name** (mandatory field): Enter a name for the site.

   - **Site description:** Provide some description about the site.

   - **Privacy settings:** Select the settings from the drop-down menu and check whether you want to keep it as Private or Public.

4. Once done, click on the **Save** option.

5. If you want to see all the site settings of your site, then click on the **View all site settings** option. After clicking on the **View all site settings** option, the **Site Settings** page appears on the screen where you can see all the site settings of your SharePoint site such as:

   - **Look and Feel**

   - **Web Designer Galleries**

   - **Site Actions**

   - **Site Administration**

   - **Site Collection Administration**

   - **Search**

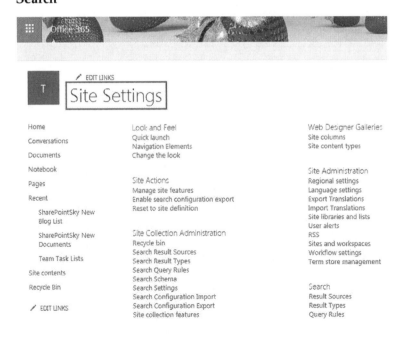

6. You can also delete the site by using the **Delete site** option as shown in the above screenshot.

Change the Site Logo in the SharePoint Online Modern Team Site

If you want to edit your site, then follow the given steps:

1. First, click on the **Site information** option from the Gear icon as shown here:

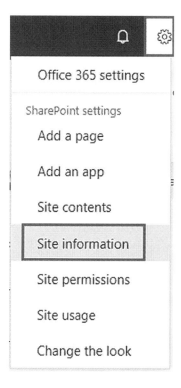

2. After clicking on the **Site information** option, the **Edit site information** page appears as shown in the following screenshot. On this page, you can see the details of your SharePoint site as follows:

- **Site logo**: If you want to change your **Site logo**, then click on the **Change** option. By clicking on this option, you can change the logo from your PC or any browser, etc.

Edit site information

Site logo

3. Once you click on **Save**, an error message appears on the screen '**We experienced a problem updating the icon. Please try again in a few minutes**' as shown in the following screenshot. This error appears on the screen when you repeatedly click on **Save**:

4. To solve this problem for the modern team site, you need to go to the Site Assets folder and upload the site logo there. It must be named __siteIcon__. jpg and must be in a .jpg format for it to work as shown in the following screenshot:

Note: The modern SharePoint logo size should be 64*64 pixel.

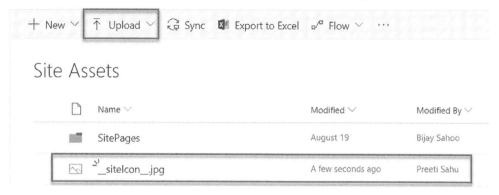

5. After a while, if you go to the **Edit site information** page, you can view the Site logo that has been changed as shown in the following screenshot:

SharePoint Online Modern Site's Site Contents Page

1. The **Site contents** page contains a list of all lists, libraries, pages and other apps and sub sites in the site. To go to the **Site content** page, click on the Gear icon from the home page and then click on the **Site contents** option as shown in the following screenshot:

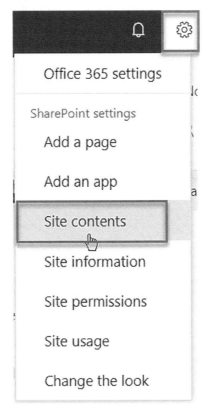

2. The following screenshot contains all the site contents such as **Documents**, **Form Template**, **SharePointSky New Documents** and so on:

At the top of the page, you can view the **+New** tab which is used to create a **New List**, **Page**, **Document Library**, **App** and **Subsite** as shown here:

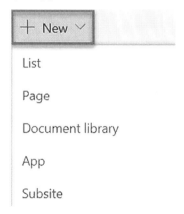

3. Then, click on **Subsites** to view the list of sub sites created under this new site:

4. Click on the eclipses (**...**) to view the options to navigate to **Remove**, **Settings**, **Details** and to remove/delete the list or library or app as shown in the following screenshot:

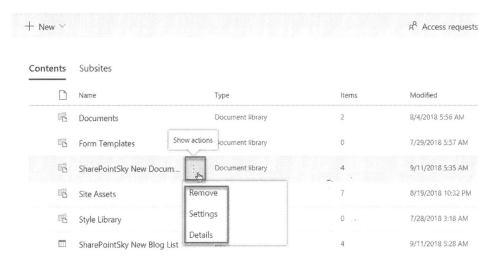

SharePoint Online Modern Team Site's Site Setting Options

In the modern SharePoint site, the **Site settings** option is not visible in the SharePoint settings:

1. To go to the **Site settings** page, click on the Gear icon from your home page and then go to the **Site contents** option:

2. In the following **Site contents** page screenshot, the **Site settings** option is located on the ribbon:

Apart from this also, you can access the settings page URL directly in the browser like below:

https://<SiteURL>/_layouts/15/settings.aspx

Example:https://onlysharepoint2013.sharepoint.com/sites/sharepointskynew/_layouts/15/settings.aspx

3. When you click on the **Site settings** option, you will see the Site settings page where the following settings of sites are available:

-   **Look and Feel**
-   **Web Designer Galleries**
-   **Site Actions**
-   **Site Administration**
-   **Site Collection Administration**
-   **Search**

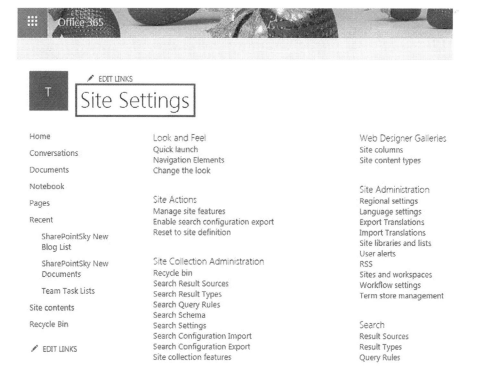

Remove the Left Navigation in Modern SharePoint

If you want to display the full modern SharePoint site Page, then you can view it by removing the left navigation from your modern SharePoint site.

In the following screenshot, you can see the left navigation which is present on the **TSInfo Technologies** SharePoint site page:

To remove this left navigation from the SharePoint site page, follow the steps given below:

1. Click on the **Edit** option as shown in the screenshot:

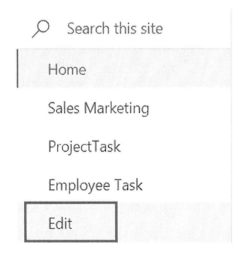

2. When you click on the **Edit** option, the **Navigation Settings** page opens which is on the **Site Settings** page. On this settings page, go to the left navigation and click on the **EDIT LINKS** button as shown in the following screenshot:

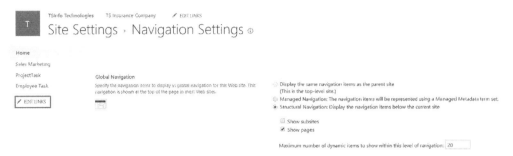

3. When you click on the **EDIT LINKS** button, the left navigation will appear as shown in the following screenshot. Remove all the links by using the cross icons. Now, the **Save** button gets enabled. After removing all the links, click on the **Save** button:

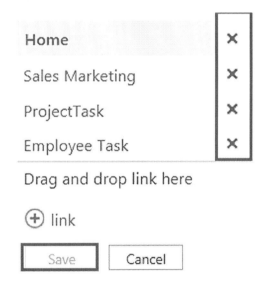

4. Here, you can view your full SharePoint site page without the left navigation as shown in the following screenshot:

Delete a Modern Team Site

You will not find any options to delete the site collection in the **Site Settings** page. It is available from the home page itself. Follow the given steps to delete the modern team site:

1. .Navigate to the home page of the site collection and click on the Gear icon. Then, go to **Site information** | **Delete site** as shown in the following screenshot:

2. When you click on the **Site information**, the **Edit Site Information** page appears on the screen. On this page, click on the **Delete Site** option which is present at the bottom of the page as shown below:

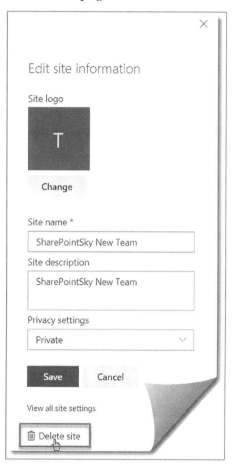

3. When you click on the **Delete site** option, it will ask you if you want to delete the existing group and all its associated resources. If you want to delete the site, then you need to check the **Yes, delete this group and all its associated resources** box.

4. After putting a check mark in the check box, the **Delete** option gets enabled. Then, click on it to delete the site:

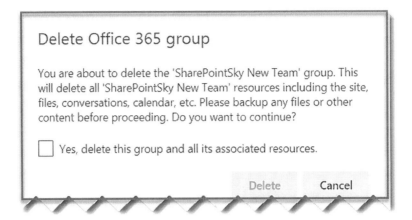

Summary

In this chapter, we learned about modern SharePoint Online team sites and how to create a modern team site in Office 365 SharePoint Online. We also learned about various site customization options like changing the site logo, left navigation customization, changing the site theme, etc., and how to delete a modern team site in Office 365.

In the next chapter, we will take a look at the modern SharePoint Online list and the various new features of modern lists.

CHAPTER 4

SharePoint Online Modern Lists

In this chapter, we will learn about a SharePoint Online modern list, the need of this modern list, and see how helpful it is to people in an organization. We will discuss the following topics:

- Different ways to create a modern SharePoint Online list
- Create a column in the modern SharePoint Online list
- Latest features of the modern SharePoint Online list

What is a Modern SharePoint Online List?

Microsoft has introduced the modern SharePoint Online list which comes with a lot of new features. Modern lists are easy to use, responsive, have a modern look and feel, and can be accessed on any devices such as a laptop, desktop, mobile, tablet, etc.

Now, the modern SharePoint list is improvised in such a way that the user can add or modify the structure of a list on same page only. This means the user doesn't need to go any other page to modify the structure. Even Microsoft has removed the classic ribbon and replaced it with a new contextual menu. Also, the position of the **List Settings** options has been changed from the ribbon to the Gear icon (Settings icon).

According to Microsoft, here are a few highlighted features of modern SharePoint Online lists:

- In modern list users can easily add columns to lists, sort, filter and can do group by easily in the same page without navigating to another page.

- Users can view, edit in bulk in the same list page without navigating to other page.

- Easily do bulk editing of list items with the **Quick edit** option in modern list.

- Automate your business processes with approvals through Microsoft flow in the modern list.

The new modern list, as shown in the following screenshot, has buttons such as **New**, **Quick edit**, **Export to Excel, Flow**, and **PowerApps**:

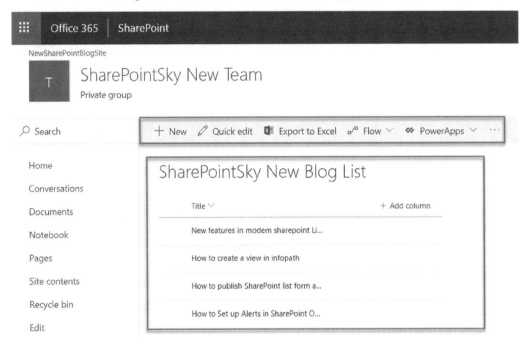

How to Create a Modern SharePoint Online List?

We can create a modern SharePoint Online list in the following two ways:

- Using the **Site contents** option
- Using the **Add an app** option

Using the Site contents Option

To create a modern SharePoint Online list, follow the given steps:

1. Go to the **Site contents** option which is present in the left navigation and as well as in the Gear icon of your home page.

2. On the **Site contents** page, you can see the **+New** option. Just click on **List** from the drop-down menu to create a new list:

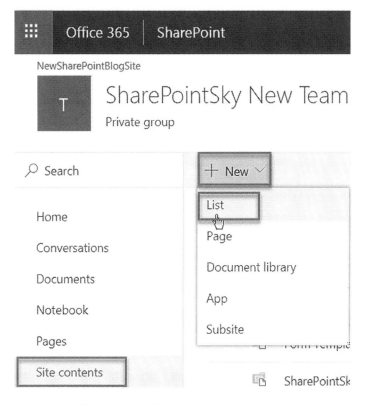

3. Then, the **Create list** page will appear on the screen where you need to fill the field values as follows:

   - **Name** (mandatory): Name of the list

   - **Description** (optional) : Description of the list

   - **Show in site navigation**: If you want to show the list in the navigation, then check the check box.

4. Click on the **Create** button which will create the modern SharePoint list as shown in the following screenshot:

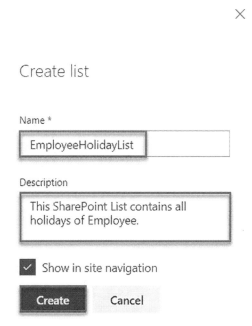

5. After creating the modern SharePoint Online list, the list will appear as shown here:

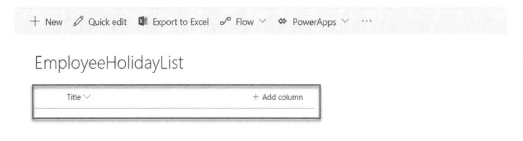

Using the Add an app Option

To create a modern SharePoint Online list using the **Add an app** option, follow the given steps:

1. Go to the Gear icon which is present at the top of the SharePoint Online modern home page and then click on the **Add an app** option as shown in the following screenshot:

2. In the **Add an app option**, you will see different templates such as:

   - **Custom List**: This creates a modern SharePoint Online custom list.

   - **Document Library**: This creates a modern SharePoint Online document library.

   - **Tasks**: This creates a modern SharePoint Online task list.

   - **Site Mailbox**: This creates a site mailbox.

3. To create a modern SharePoint Online list, click on the **Custom List** option as shown here:

4. After clicking on the **Custom List** option, the **Adding Custom List** dialogue box appears on the screen where you need to give a unique list name. Then, click on the **Create** option to create a new modern SharePoint Online list:

5. The following screenshot represents the new modern SharePoint Online list which looks attractive:

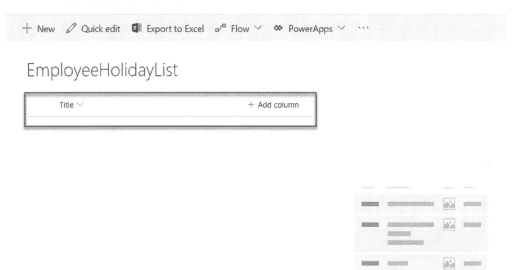

6. When you click on **Advanced options** of the **Adding Custom List** dialogue box, it displays a page where you need to enter the **Name** as well as **Description** and then click on the **Create** button:

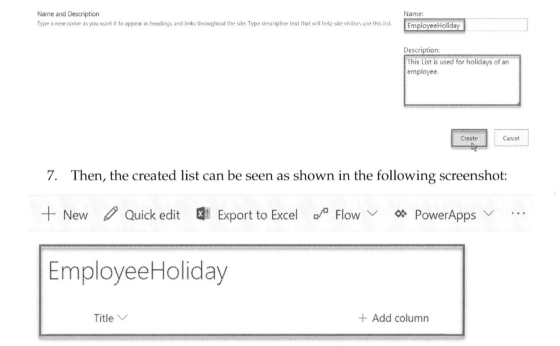

7. Then, the created list can be seen as shown in the following screenshot:

The Modern SharePoint Online List features

Microsoft office 365 has added a lot of features in the modern SharePoint online list which are beneficial for users. They are as follows:

No Ribbon is Available in the Modern SharePoint Online List

1. Unlike the classic SharePoint Online list, there is no ribbon in the SharePoint Online modern list. The ribbon is replaced by the command bar.

2. In the command bar, you will find options to add **New Item** (new), **Quick edit** (option to edit the entire list as Excel), **Export to Excel**, **Flow** (create workflows using Microsoft Flow), **PowerApps** (create apps using Microsoft PowerApps), **Alert me**, **Manage my alerts** as shown in the following screenshot:

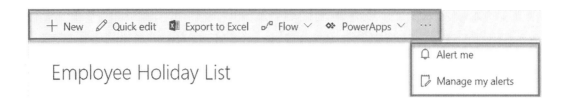

Access List Settings Page in the Modern SharePoint Online List

As there is no ribbon in a modern list, you can access the **List settings** page from the Gear icon | **List settings**:

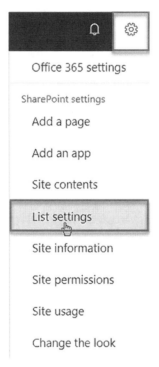

Add a Column in a Modern SharePoint Online List

Microsoft has made it very easy to add or create a column in a modern SharePoint online list. We can add a column on the same page without navigating to another page.

We can add single or multiple columns in the modern SharePoint list as follows:

1. To create a column, click on the **+Add column** button in the list as shown in the following screenshot:

2. Here, you can see different types of column options such as:

    *   A single line of text
    *   Multiple lines of text
    *   Number
    *   Yes/No
    *   Person
    *   Date
    *   Choice
    *   Hyperlink
    *   Picture
    *   Currency

3. If you need to add any other type of column, click on the **More...** option which opens the classic add column page.

4. From the drop-down menu, choose the type of column you want.

5. For example, I have chosen a **Date type** column to store **Holiday Date**.

6. After choosing the type of column, the **Create Column** dialog box will open. It has the following fields which need to be filled (Below properties are for a DateTime column, if you are using any other column type then the properties will differ):

    *   **Name** (Mandatory): The name of the field.
    *   **Description** (Optional): The description of the field.
    *   **Type**: Select the type of column you want from the drop-down menu.
    *   **Include Time**: Enable or disable it to include time in the notification.
    *   **Friendly format**: Enable or disable it to include time in the notification.
    *   **Default value**: Select a default value from that dropdown and check whether you want to give any specific date or none.

- **Use calculate the value**: Check box.

- **Require that this column contains information**: Enable/Disable.

- **Enforce unique values**: Enable/Disable.

- **Add to all content types**: Enable/Disable.

- **Column validation**: Specify the formula that you want to use to validate the data in this column when new items are saved to this list.

7. After entering all the column field values, just click on the **Save** option to save the **List column** as shown in the following screenshot:

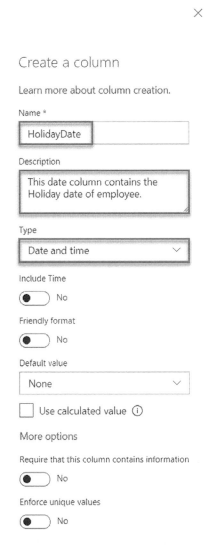

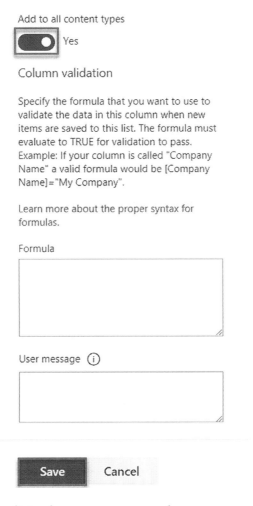

Add to all content types

Yes

Column validation

Specify the formula that you want to use to
validate the data in this column when new
items are saved to this list. The formula must
evaluate to TRUE for validation to pass.
Example: If your column is called "Company
Name" a valid formula would be [Company
Name]="My Company".

Learn more about the proper syntax for
formulas.

Formula

User message ⓘ

Save   Cancel

8. After saving the list column, a message column was created will be displayed
    in your list as shown below:

Employee Holiday List

| Title ∨ | HolidayDate ∨ | + Add column |

HolidayDate was created ✕

Add a column in Your Desired Place by Using the + Symbol

You can also create a column in your desired place by using the + symbol. This is a new look to create a column in the Modern SharePoint list or library.

To get the + symbol, just put the cursor at any starting or ending point of the column name. When you click on the + symbol, it will display all the types of columns and you can create a column easily.

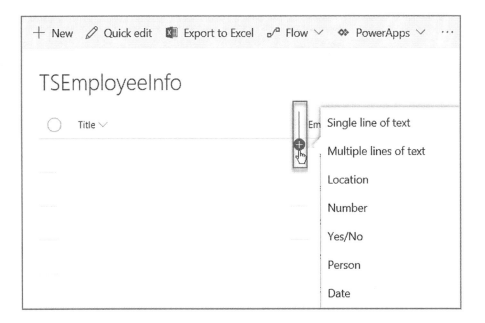

List Details Pane

The SharePoint Online modern list provides the list details pane from where a user can see recent activities of the list as well as activities of the individual list items.

To view list level activities, click on the details pane icon which is present at the top of the SharePoint Online modern list.

Make sure not to select any individual list item.

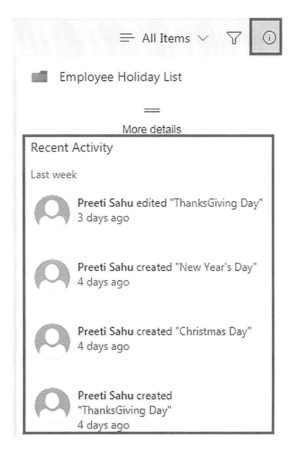

If you select a particular list item from the modern list in the list details pane, it will show you the details of that particular item as shown in the following screenshot.

I have selected the list item as **Independence Day**, so it displays the details of **Independence Day** as follows:

- **Title**
- **Holiday Date**
- **Holiday Confirmation**
- **Attachments**

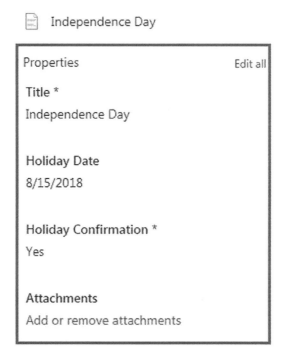

Change the Column Width Easily

In the classic SharePoint list, there is no out-of-the-box way to resize the width of a list column. To customize it, we need to write scripts or code. But now SharePoint provides a new feature to increase or decrease the column width. We can now simply drag a column to increase or decrease its width.

Here, in the following screenshot, you can see the arrow mark of **HolidayDate** which helps you to increase or decrease the size of the column width:

Drag and Drop Any Column to Any Position

Microsoft has provided a new feature where you can drag and drop your desired column to your desired position in SharePoint list/library. Let's see the following example:

In the following screenshot, I have two columns **EmployeeJoiningDate** and **EmployeeSalary**. I just want to drag and drop the **EmployeeSalary** column after the **EmployeeEmailID** column. So, to do this, I dragged the **EmployeeSalary** column and dropped it at the **EmployeeJoiningDate** column.

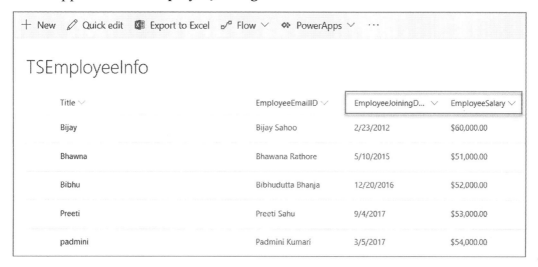

After dragging and dropping the column, you can view the changes as shown in the following screenshot:

Now, to save the view as the **EmployeeSalary** column, click on the **title** bar which is present in the command bar. Click on **Save view as** as shown below:

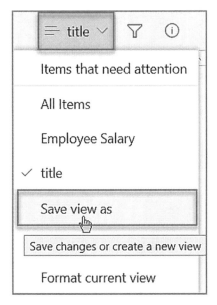

You need to save the current view or type a new name of the changed field. Here, I have changed the **EmployeeSalary** field, so I saved the view as **EmployeeSalary**. If you want to make this a public view, then check the check box of **Make this a public view** and click on **Save** as shown below:

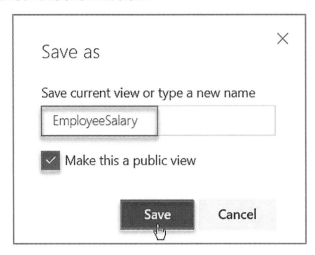

Now, you can view it as **EmployeeSalary** in the command bar.

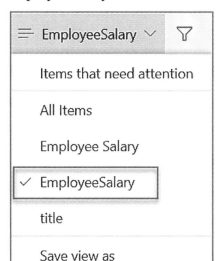

Create an Item in a Modern SharePoint Online List

Go to the **+New** option which is present at the top of the list. Then, the **New item** page will be displayed where you need to enter all the field values.

1. The **New item** page contains the following fields:

    *   **Title** (mandatory field)

    *   **HolidayDate** (optional field)

    *   **Attachments**: If you want to attach any files/documents, then click on **Add attachments** otherwise it's optional.

2. After entering all the field values, click on the **Save** option to save the list item:

3. Similarly, you can create multiple numbers of items in the modern SharePoint Online list. I have created multiple number of items list as shown in the following screenshot:

Employee Holiday List

Title ∨	HolidayDate ∨
Independence Day	8/15/2018
Labor Day	9/7/2018
ThanksGiving Day	11/27/2018
Christmas Day	12/25/2018
New Year's Day	1/1/2019

Edit the List Item in the Modern SharePoint Online List

1. To edit, update or modify the list item, modern SharePoint Online provides the option **Quick edit**. By using this option, you can modify your list item very quickly. Hence, its name is **Quick edit** and it also helps saves time.

2. To edit the list item, just go to the **Quick edit** option which is present at the top of the modern SharePoint Online list as shown in the following screenshot:

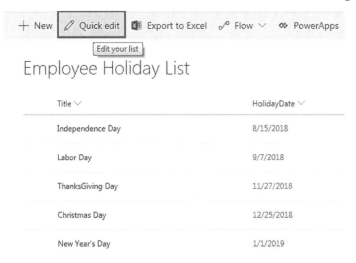

+ New   ⬠ Quick edit   ⬛ Export to Excel   ⌀° Flow ∨   ✪ PowerApps

Edit your list

Employee Holiday List

Title ∨	HolidayDate ∨
Independence Day	8/15/2018
Labor Day	9/7/2018
ThanksGiving Day	11/27/2018
Christmas Day	12/25/2018
New Year's Day	1/1/2019

3. After clicking on the **Quick edit** option, the list item will be displayed as shown here. Now, you can modify or edit your list item.

4. After editing/modifying the list item, just click on the **Exit quick edit** option which is present at the top of the list to exit the quick edit:

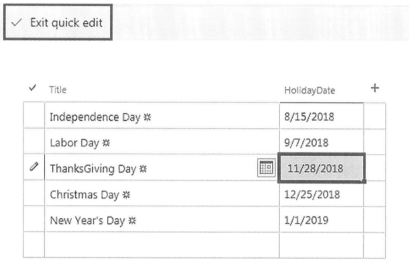

5. Now, in the following screenshot, you can see that your list item has been modified/updated.

6. Similarly, if you want to modify all your list items at a time, then you can do it in the same way as mentioned above:

Employee Holiday List

Title ∨	HolidayDate ∨
Independence Day	8/15/2018
Labor Day	9/7/2018
ThanksGiving Day	11/28/2018
Christmas Day	12/25/2018
New Year's Day	1/1/2019

Export to Excel (Browser Other than Internet Explorer)

Previously, we can use the Export to Excel functionality only in Internet explorer, now you can use in other browsers.

1. The modern SharePoint Online list provides the feature **Export to Excel** with a new look. This feature is present at the top of the modern list.

2. Click on the **Export to Excel** option. Then, the **Save as** page appears on the screen where you need to save the file by giving the **File name** as shown in the following screenshot:

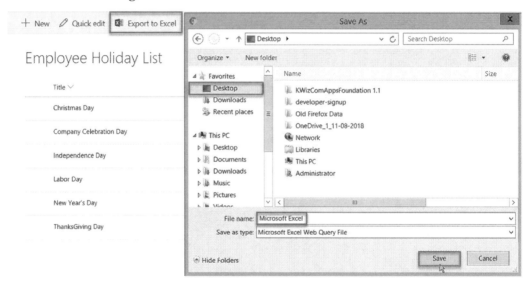

3. When you open the Excel file, you will see the data or items in the Excel sheet:

Create Microsoft Flow

Microsoft Flow is a service comes with Office 365 and tightly integrated with SharePoint Online lists and libraries. It is an automated business process of an organization which helps to allow workflow based on certain triggers and actions.

For example, when you add a new item to the modern SharePoint list, a customized email will be sent to an individual for reviewing.

Similarly, when you upload a document to the modern SharePoint document library, a customized email will be sent to your manager for approving or rejecting the document.

If you are new to Microsoft Flow, then read a detailed article on Microsoft Flow on how it works at https://www.sharepointsky.com/microsoft-flow/.

In the following screenshot, you can see the **Flow** feature which is present at the top of the modern SharePoint Online list. When you click on the **Flow** option, you can see the following options:

- **Create a flow**: This is used to create a new flow.
- **See your flows**: This is used to view your flows you had created earlier.
- **Configure flows**: This is used to configure your flows.

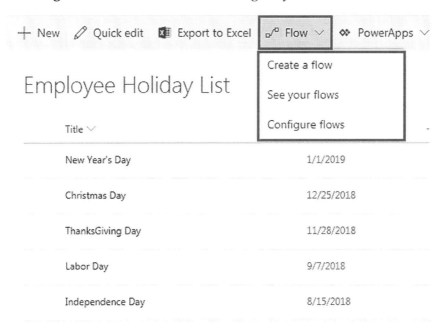

PowerApps

PowerApps is another service by Microsoft, which can be accessible directly from SharePoint Online list. By using PowerApps, you can create a new app, as well as customize forms in SharePoint Online modern lists.

To create a new PowerApps, follow the given steps:

1. **Create an app**: Go to the **PowerApps** option which is present at the top of the list. Then, click on the **Create an app** option from the drop-down menu:

2. After clicking on the **Create an app** option, the **Create an app** page will be displayed where you need to enter the name of the PowerApps in the **Name** field. Then, click on **Create** to create your new PowerApps:

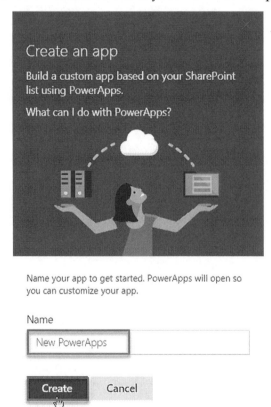

3. **Customize forms**: Go to the **PowerApps** option which is present at the top of the list. Then, click on the **Customized forms** option from the drop-down menu:

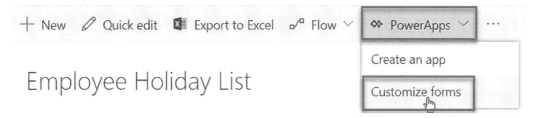

4. When you click on the **Customized forms** option, the **PowerApps** page appears which is used for designing purpose: PowerApps is not the scope of this book, but you can see some PowerApps examples in https://www. sharepointsky.com/category/microsoft-powerapps/

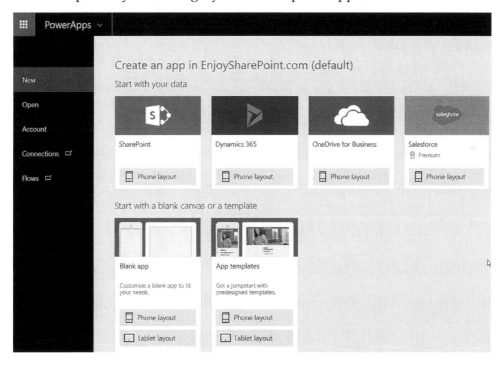

Set Up Alerts in the SharePoint Online modern list Using the Alert me Feature

The modern SharePoint list provides the **Alert me** feature. When someone makes any changes in any file, folder or document in your document library or list, you get an alert or notification that your files or documents have been changed by someone:

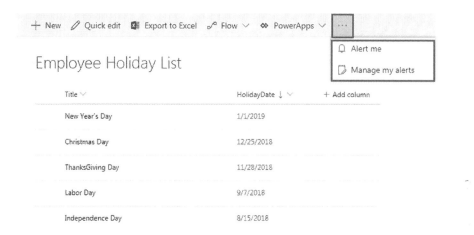

Share an Item in the Modern SharePoint Online List

The modern SharePoint Online provides the new **Share** feature with a new look. This **Share** option is used for sharing the details of a list item from one person to another person or another user:

1. To share the item, just select the SharePoint Online list item which you want to share and then go to the **Share** option which is present at the top of the modern SharePoint Online list and on the right-hand side of the selected list item as shown in the following screenshot:

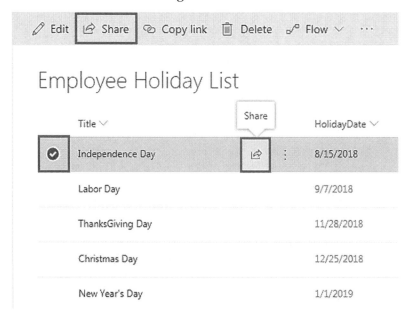

2. When you click on the **Share** option, the **Send Link** page appears on the screen where you need to enter the username with whom you want to share the list item.

3. Enter the username with whom you want to share the list item. You can enter multiple numbers of usernames by using the **Add another** option.

4. There is a **Subject** field also available where you can type the subject details about the list item. Then, click on the **Send** option as shown in the following screenshot:

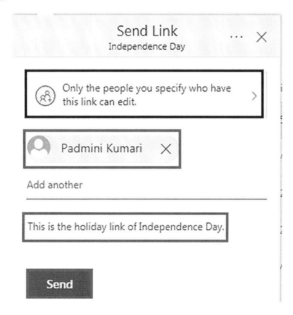

5. After sending the list item to another user, a status message will show you the link of the selected list item sent as shown in the following screenshot:

6. In the previous screenshot, you can see the **Only the people you specify who have this link can edit** option which is highlighted in black color. If you go to this option, the **Link settings** page will appear on the screen.

7. The following screenshot represents the **Link settings** page which specifies whom you want to allow to edit or not to the user. If you want to allow the user to edit, then check the check box of **Allow editing** (by default, it is checked). Then, click on **Apply**:

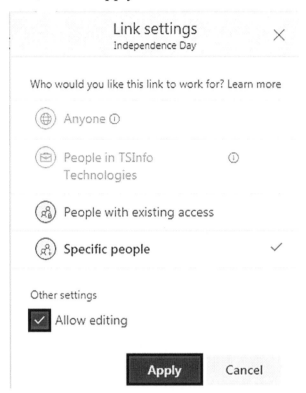

Copy Link and Outlook features in the Modern SharePoint List

1. These are the features provided by the modern SharePoint list/library. The **Copy Link** and **Outlook** options are present in the **Share** feature of SharePoint list item which I discussed earlier.

2. When you share the files/documents to another person, you can see the **Copy Link** and Outlook options in the **Send Links** page which is shown in the following screenshot:

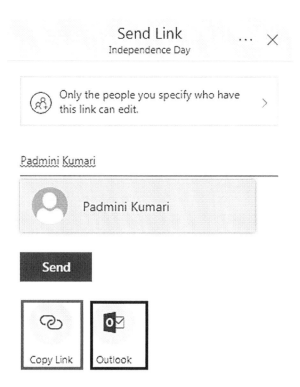

3. When you click on **Copy Link** (highlighted in red), you will see a **Copy** status of that particular selected list item as shown below. This means your selected list item link is copied.

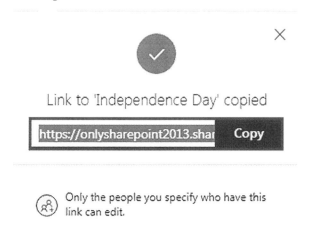

4. When you click on **Outlook** (highlighted in black), you will see the **Creating Shareable link…** status of that particular selected list item as shown in the following screenshot:

Stop sharing in the Modern SharePoint Online List Item

Stop sharing is a new feature of the modern SharePoint list which was not available in the classic SharePoint list.

1. If you want to stop the sharing of a particular list item to any user, then select a list item and click on the **Share** option which is present at the right-hand side of the selected item and also at the top of the SharePoint list:

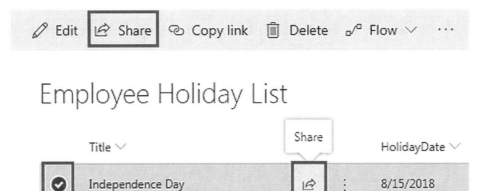

2. Then, the **Send Link** page appears on the screen. On this page, you will see the **...** option present at the top of the page. Just click on the **...** option and again click on **Manage Access** as shown in the following screenshot:

3. Now, the **Manage Access** page appears on the screen. On this page, you can see all the users with whom you want to share the list item. Here, you can also give the user permissions to anyone by using the **Grant Access** option which is present at the top of the page.

4. If you stop the sharing, it will disable all the links giving access to this item and remove all the people with direct access except the owners. Then, click on to the **Stop sharing** option as shown in the following screenshot:

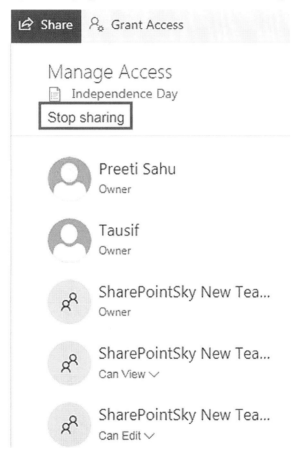

5. Once you click on the **Stop sharing** option, it will disable all the links and remove all the people with direct access except owners:

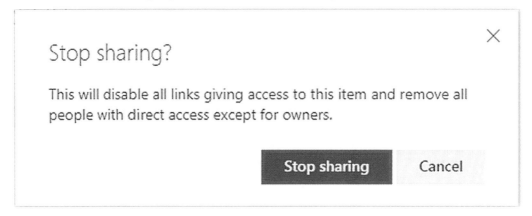

Order the List column (date column) as Older to Newer and it's Vice Versa in the Modern SharePoint List

Order is a new feature of the modern SharePoint list where you can change the order depending on your existing column. There are two types of orders present in the order feature:

- **Older to newer**
- **Newer to older**

Here, I will show you the order change of the date column example below.

Older to Newer

Let's take a column which should be a date. Click on the column and select the **Older to newer** option from the drop-down menu highlighted in red as shown below.

1. Once the selection is done, you can see the proper order **Older to newer** of the list item highlighted in black as shown below:

Employee Holiday List

Title ∨	HolidayDate ↑ ∨	+ Add column
Independence Day	8/15/2018	
Labor Day	9/7/2018	
ThanksGiving Day	11/28/2018	
Christmas Day	12/25/2018	
New Year's Day	1/1/2019	

✓ Older to newer

Newer to older

Filter by

Group by HolidayDate

Column settings   >

Newer to Older

1. Similarly, like the **Older to Newer** option, click on the date column and select the **Newer to older** option from the drop-down menu highlighted in red as shown below.

2. Once the selection is done, you can see the proper order Newer to older of the list item highlighted in black as shown below:

Employee Holiday List

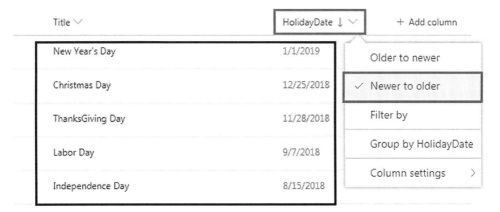

Title ∨	HolidayDate ↓ ∨	+ Add column
New Year's Day	1/1/2019	
Christmas Day	12/25/2018	
ThanksGiving Day	11/28/2018	
Labor Day	9/7/2018	
Independence Day	8/15/2018	

Older to newer

✓ Newer to older

Filter by

Group by HolidayDate

Column settings   >

Filter by the Column

Filter by is another new feature in the modern SharePoint list which is used to filter the column value.

1. For filtering the value of a column, click on a specific column which you want to filter and then click on the **Filter by** option from the drop-down column as shown in the following screenshot:

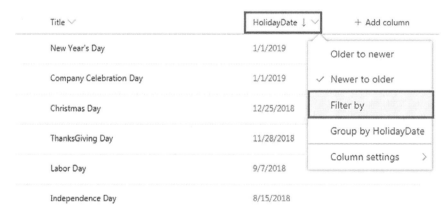

2. Then, the **Filter by** page will appear on the right-hand side of your existing list page where you need to give the filter value for whatever you want to filter as shown in the following screenshot:

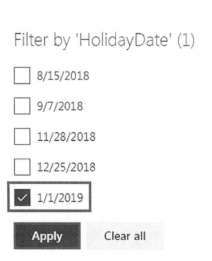

3. Now, you need to select a specific title you want to filter as shown in following screenshot. Then, click on the **Reset** option to view the filter value:

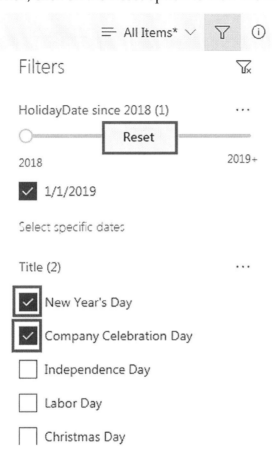

4. Here, in the following screenshot, you can see the specific date filter value:

Employee Holid... > New Year's Day, Company Celebration Day

Title ▽ ∨	HolidayDate ↓ ∨	+ Add column
New Year's Day	1/1/2019	
Company Celebration Day	1/1/2019	

Mandatory Field Validation Notification

Another new feature you can see in the modern SharePoint list is the **mandatory field validation notification**. Let's see the following example:

1. Here, I have created a column by using the **+ Add column** option which should be the **Choice** column as shown in the following screenshot:

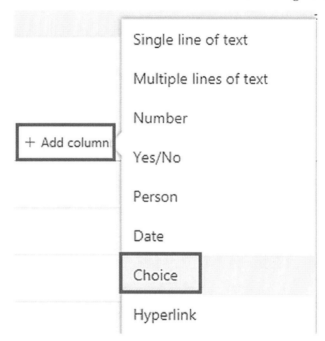

2. After clicking on the **Choice** option, the **Create a column** page appear on the screen where you need to enter the details of a column as follows:

- **Name**: Single line of text which should be a mandatory field
- **Description**: Multiline of text
- **Type: Choice**
- **Choices: Yes/No**

3. Then, set the **Default value** option as **None**. In **More options**, select the **Drop-Down Menu** as **Display Choice** and also enable the option as **Require that this column contains information**. Then, click on the **Save** option to save the details of the column:

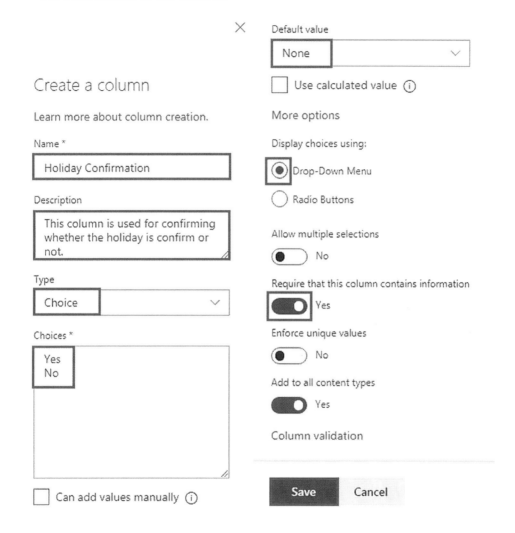

4. Now, the new choice column is created and named **Holiday Confirmation**. Here, in the following screenshot, I did not fill the choice column. So, the **Required info** notification appears in the columns. That's why a yellow mark mandatory field validation appears on the right-hand side of the list:

Employee Holiday List

Title ∨	HolidayDate ∨	Holiday Confirmation ∨
Independence Day	8/15/2018	ⓘ Required info
Labor Day	9/7/2018	ⓘ Required info
ThanksGiving Day	11/28/2018	ⓘ Required info
Christmas Day	12/25/2018	ⓘ Required info
New Year's Day	1/1/2019	ⓘ Required info
Company Celebration Day	1/1/2019	ⓘ Required info

5. So, to fill the choice column as **Holiday Confirmation**, just click on **Required info** as shown in the following screenshot:

Employee Holiday List

Title ∨			HolidayDate ∨	Holiday Confirmation ∨
◯ Independence Day	⬆	⋮	8/15/2018	ⓘ Required info

6. Then, a **Setting pane** page will appear on the screen where you need to enter the column details of that particular item. Here, just go to **Holiday Confirmation** and select the choice field as the **Yes/No** option from the drop-down menu as per your requirement. Then, it will be saved automatically in the list:

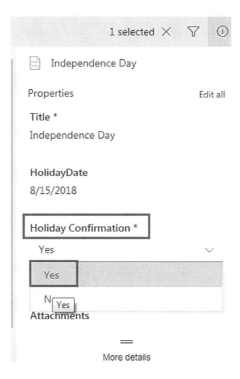

7. In the following screenshot, since I have filled the **Holiday Confirmation** column values, the yellow mark does not appear in those items. So, if you fill all the item values, the yellow mark will not be displayed any further.

Employee Holiday List

Title ⌄	HolidayDate ⌄	Holiday Confirmation ⌄
Independence Day	8/15/2018	Yes
Labor Day	9/7/2018	Yes
ThanksGiving Day	11/28/2018	ⓘ Required info
Christmas Day	12/25/2018	ⓘ Required info
New Year's Day	1/1/2019	ⓘ Required info
Company Celebration Day	1/1/2019	ⓘ Required info

Easily View Items without any Next Previous buttons in the SharePoint Online Modern List

Now users can view items without any Next, Previous buttons in the modern SharePoint list. The pagination in the modern UI is based on the View Height. i.e., instead of clicking the next and previous buttons, the content of the list loads based on the visible section on the browser.

In the classic SharePoint list, when you scroll down the list page, the list page opens by clicking on the **Next Page** or **Previous Page** option.

But in the modern SharePoint list, when you scroll down the list page, the list page loads automatically.

Save View in the Modern SharePoint List

The modern SharePoint list provides the **save view** feature to create a view in one click without navigating to any page:

1. To see the view of the **Save view as** option, first change something in your list column. I have changed the order of the title column **A to Z** as shown in the following screenshot:

Employee Holiday List

Title ↑ ∨		Holiday Date ∨	Holiday Confirmation ∨
Christm	✓ A to Z	12/25/2018	Yes
Compa	Z to A	1/1/2019	Yes
Indepe	Filter by	8/15/2018	Yes
Labor [	Column settings ＞	9/7/2018	Yes
New Year's Day		1/1/2019	Yes
ThanksGiving Day		11/28/2018	Yes

2. Now, go to the **All Items*** option which is present at the top of the modern SharePoint list. Then, click on the **Save view as** option as shown in the following screenshot:

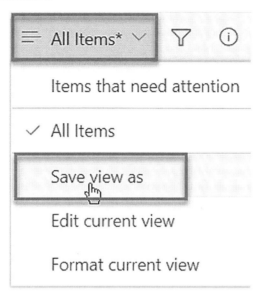

3. After clicking on the **Save view as** option, the **Save as** page appears on the screen where you need to type a new name to save the current view. Check the checkbox of **Make this a public view** and click on **Save** to save the new view:

4. Once the view is saved, you can see the current view as **New items** which is newly saved as shown below:

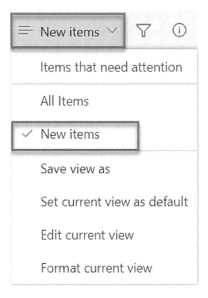

Group by in one click in the SharePoint Online Modern List

By using the **Group by** option of the modern SharePoint list, you can now do **Group by** from the column itself without navigating to any page:

1. If you want to **Group by** any list column, go to that particular list column and click on **Group by** (that specific column name) from the drop-down column as shown in the following screenshot:

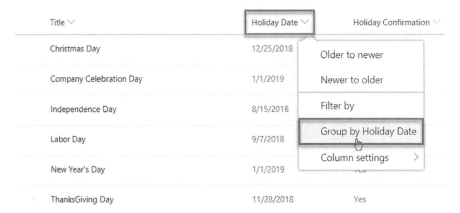

2. Then, you will see **Group by** (with that specific column) as shown in the following screenshot:

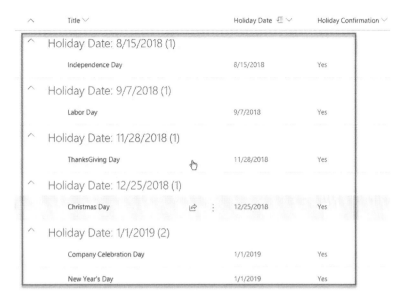

Open ECB Menu Just on a Right Click

A new feature has been released in the modern SharePoint document list. The feature defines that when you right click at any place of the document library page, the ECB menu opens directly.

An ECB menu appears for each item or file in SharePoint list or document library like below which has come actions associated with it.

When a user needs to open the ECB menu, there is no need to go to any other option. It will directly open at any place of the list page just on a right click as shown in the following screenshot:

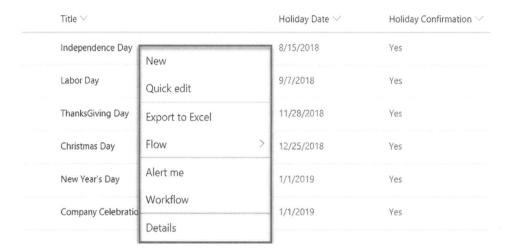

Items that need attention

Recently, Microsoft has released a new feature **Items that need attention** which is present in the modern SharePoint list. Earlier, it was not present in the classic SharePoint list.

We are familiar with the necessary metadata and sometimes we forget to assign the metadata. So, to resolve this issue, the attention view can be used.

1. If you forget to any value to any column field, then a yellow colored mandatory field validation notification occurs in the SharePoint list as shown in the following screenshot:

2. If you want to keep your attention with that mandatory field value, then go to the **All Items** option which is present at the top of the list. Then, click on the **Items that need attention** feature.

3. After clicking on the **Items that need attention** feature, you will able to see the **Missing info** column value as shown in the following screenshot:

4. To resolve this missing info column, click on the specific **Missing info** column of that item and then in the list pane, go to the missing column and edit the value you want and it will be saved automatically in the list:

5. After saving the column field value, the missing info will be resolved as shown in the following screenshot:

Display user details on mouse hover

Microsoft has released a new feature in the modern SharePoint Online list and the modern SharePoint document library.

If you hover your mouse on a particular user, then it will show you the details of the user as shown below.

Using this new feature, you can directly open the **Send email** box (to send any email to another user), chat box (to chat with another user) and LinkedIn (to view the LinkedIn details):

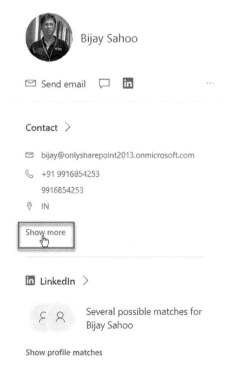

If you want to show more details about the user, then click on the **Show more** option as shown in the following screenshot:

Once you click on the **Show more** option, the **User Profile Page** appears on the screen where you can see all the information about that specific user. There are five tabs present as follows:

- **Contact**: This shows all the contact information about the user like **Email**, **Chat**, **Mobile**, and **Work phone.**

- **About**: This shows the details about the user.

- **Organization**: This shows the user organization.

- **Files**: This shows the recent used files by the user.

- **LinkedIn**: This shows the information of LinkedIn.

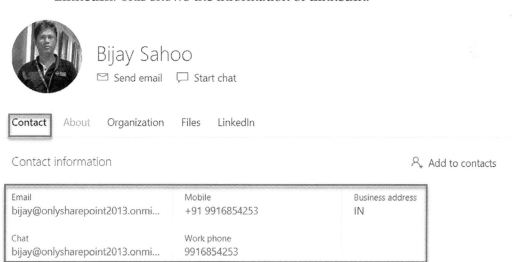

If you go to the **Files** tab, you will see all the recent files/documents used by the user recently.

Also, you can copy each file/document by using the link icon which is present at the right-hand side of each and every document as shown in the following screenshot:

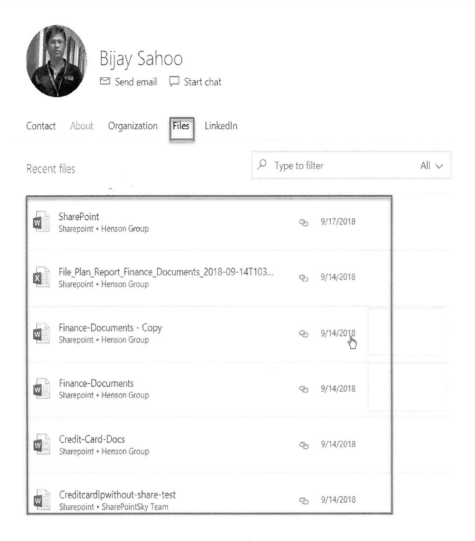

Summary

In this chapter, we learned about SharePoint Online modern lists, how to create a modern list, various new and very useful features of modern SharePoint lists. In the next chapter, we will take a look at SharePoint Online modern document libraries and various useful features of document libraries.

CHAPTER 5

Explore SharePoint Online Modern Document Libraries

In this chapter, we will learn about the modern SharePoint Online document library, the need of this document library and see how helpful it is for people in an organization. In this modern SharePoint Online document library, we will discuss the following points:

- Different ways to create a modern SharePoint Online document library
- Create a column in the modern SharePoint Online document library
- Latest features of the modern SharePoint Online document library

Like modern SharePoint lists, there are new features added to modern SharePoint document libraries as well by Microsoft.

The modern SharePoint online document library helps to store all documents, files, and folders related to a specific project of an organization.

The new document library has a few significant features as follows:

- Document details pane
- Select and download as a Zip
- Copy/Move to selected documents from one site to another site
- Tiles view of document

The new library has buttons like **New, Upload, Sync, Export to Excel, Flow** and so on as shown in the following screenshot:

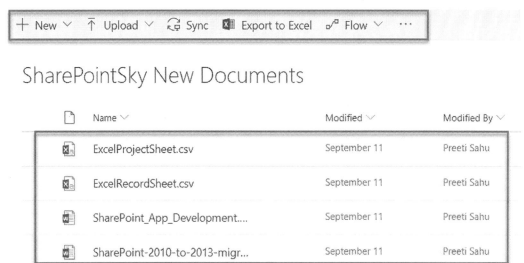

How to Create a Modern SharePoint Online Document Library?

We can create a modern SharePoint Online document library in the following two ways:

- Using the **Site contents** option
- Using the **Add an app** option

Let's discuss how to create a modern SharePoint Online document library using these options.

Using the Site contents option

To create a modern SharePoint document library, follow these steps:

1. Go to the **Site contents** option which is present in the left navigation and the Gear icon of your home page.

2. On the **Site contents** page, you can see the **+New** option. Just click on the **Document library** option from the dropdown to create a new library:

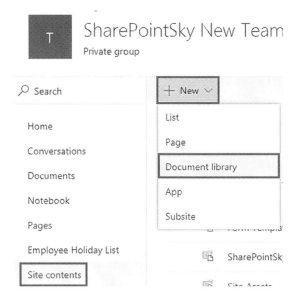

3. Then, the **Create document library** page appears on the screen where you need to fill the fields as follows:

    - **Name**: This is a mandatory field.

    - **Description**: This is an optional field.

    - **Shown in site navigation**: If you want to show the list in the navigation, then put a check in the check box.

4. Click on the **Create** option to create the modern SharePoint document library as shown in the following screenshot:

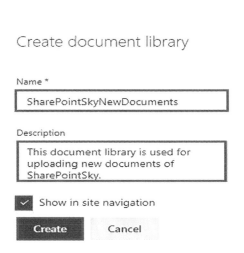

5. After creating the modern SharePoint document library, it will look as shown in the following screenshot:

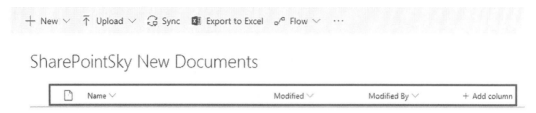

Using the Add an app option

To create a modern SharePoint document library, follow the given steps:

1. Go to the Gear icon which is present at the top of the SharePoint Online modern home page and then click on the **Add an app** option as shown in the following screenshot:

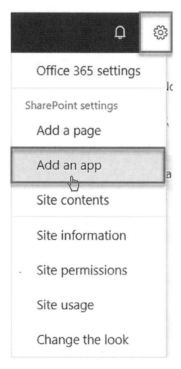

2. In the **Add an app option**, we have different templates such as:

- **Document Library**: To create a modern SharePoint Online document library

- **Custom List**: To create a modern SharePoint Online custom list

- **Tasks**: To create a modern SharePoint Online task list
- **Site Mailbox**: To create a site mailbox

3. To create a modern SharePoint Online library, click on **Document Library**:

4. When you click on the **Document Library** template, the **Adding Document Library** dialogue box appears on the screen where you need to give a unique library name and then click on the **Create** option to create a new modern SharePoint Online document library:

5. The following screenshot shows the modern SharePoint Online document library which looks very attractive:

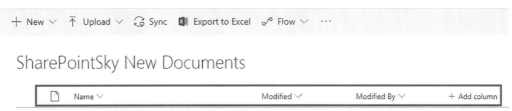

6. If you click on **Advanced options** of the **Adding Document Library** dialogue box, a page will be displayed where you need to fill the details in the following fields:

- **Name and Description**: Here you need to provide the name and give description of the document library.

- **Document Version History**: Specify whether a version needs to be created each time you edit a file in the document library

- **Document Template**: Select a document template to determine the default template for all the new files created in the document library.

7. And then, click on the **Create** button:

8. The created document library is shown in the following screenshot:

SharePoint Online Modern Document Library Features

Microsoft rolled out exciting features in the SharePoint document library, which are discussed in the following sections.

Quickly access the library settings page

Previously, in the classic SharePoint document library, the **Library setting** option was present in the ribbon. But in the modern SharePoint document library, the **Library settings** option is present at the top of the page which looks like a Gear icon.

Easily create a column in the modern SharePoint document library

As in the modern SharePoint list, we can add multiple number of columns in the modern SharePoint document library.

To create a column in the modern SharePoint document library, follow the steps given below:

1. Go to the **+ Add column** option which is present on the right-hand side of the title column (by default in the SharePoint library). Here, you can see a number of column options:

   - **Single line of text**

   - **Multiple lines of text**

   - **Number**

   - **Yes/No**

   - **Person**

   - **Date**

   - **Choice**

   - **Hyperlink**

   - **Picture**

   - **Currency**

2. From these columns, you can choose your required column, depending on your library. Here, in the following screenshot, I have chosen my column as **Person** which is used to approve the documents:

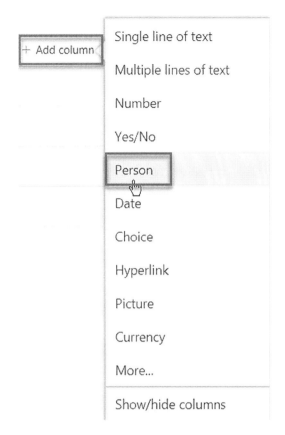

3. Then, the **Create a column** page will appear on the right-hand side of your existing page. On this page, you need to enter all the field values of the new columns as follows:

- **Name**: It is a mandatory field
- **Description**: It is an optional field
- **Type**: Select the type of column you want from the drop-down menu
- **Allow selection of Groups** : Enable/Disable
- **Allow multiple selections**: Enable/Disable
- **Require that this column contains information**: Enable/Disable
- **Enforce unique values**: Enable/Disable
- **Add to all content types**: Enable/Disable

4. After entering all the column field values, just click on the **Save** option to save the library column as shown in the following screenshot:

5. After saving the library column, a message **column was created** will be displayed in your library and the column will be created as shown in the following screenshot:

Change the column width

In the classic SharePoint document library, to change the width of a particular column, we need to add a lot of scripts or code.

Now, Microsoft has made this very easy in the SharePoint Online modern document library. It provides an easy way to **Change Column Width**. Users can increase or decrease the width of a library column by using the drag option.

Here, in the following screenshot, you can see the arrow mark of the **Modified** column which is used to increase or decrease the column width:

Easily upload a document in the modern SharePoint Online library

The **Upload** feature is present in both SharePoint classic and modern. The classic SharePoint library upload feature is like the very old version.

That's why Microsoft developed a new upload feature in the modern SharePoint library which looks better.

Follow the given steps to upload a document in the document library:

1. Go to the **Upload** option which is present at the top of the library.

2. Then, choose your particular **File/Folder/Template** from the upload drop-down option as shown in the following screenshot:

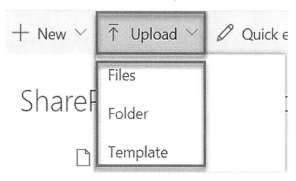

3. After uploading the document from the specific **File/Folder/Template**, you can see the status as **Document (Document name) is now available** and your document will be available in the document library as shown in the given screenshot:

Note: Read **Add template** section to know more about Template option.

Easily quick edit bulk data

To edit, update or modify the library/list item, Microsoft has provided the **Quick edit** option to both classic and modern SharePoint document library/list. But in the modern SharePoint library, this **Quick edit** option looks better than in the classic SharePoint library.

By using this option, you can modify your whole library documents very quickly. Hence, its name is **Quick edit** and it also helps to time save time. Follow the given steps to edit bulk data:

1. For editing the documents, just go to the **Quick edit** option which is present at the top of the modern SharePoint library as shown in the following screenshot:

2. After clicking on the **Quick edit** option, the document library will display the page as shown in the following screenshot. Now, you can modify or edit your documents you want.

3. After editing/modifying the documents, just click on to the **Exit quick edit** option which is present at the top of the library to exit the quick edit:

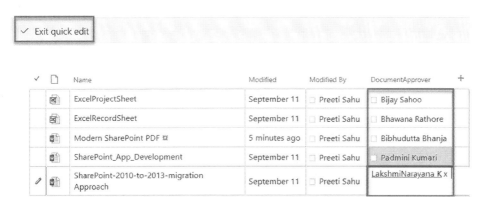

4. Now, in the following screenshot, you can see your document that is modified/updated:

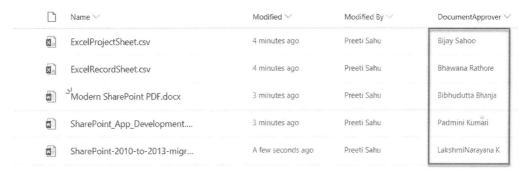

5. Similarly, if you want to modify all your documents at a time, you can do it in the same way as I mentioned earlier.

Document Details Pane

The SharePoint Online modern document library provides a new feature named **document details pane** which is not present in classic SharePoint.

By using this document pane, a user can see their recent activities on individual files and documents, or whole library:

1. In the following screenshot, you can see the library level activities by using the details pane icon which is present at the top of the document library. Without selecting a document if you just click on the details pane icon, you will be able to see the activities for the document library:

2. If you select a particular document from the document library, it will show you the details of that particular document in the document details pane as shown in the following screenshot. I have selected the first Excel document, so it displays the details of the Excel document in the following format:

- **Type**
- **Modified**
- **Path**
- **Size**

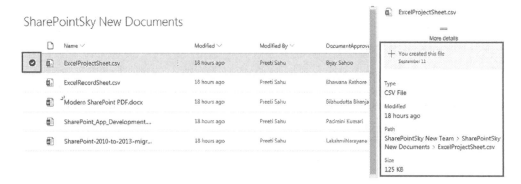

Tiles View of Documents

1. In the modern SharePoint document library, you can see your documents in different views like **List**, **Compact list** and so on. In between all the views, the **Tiles** view is a new feature which is provided by the modern SharePoint library.

2. To select this **Tiles** view, go to the **All Documents** option which is present at the top of the document library. Then, click on the **Tiles** option as shown in the following screenshot:

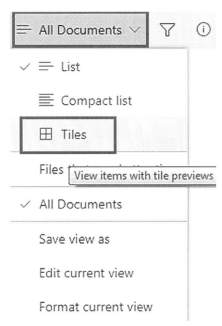

3. Here, in the following screenshot, you can see the **Tiles** view of all documents that are present in the modern SharePoint document library:

SharePointSky New Documents

4. Also if you want to display your library column with the **Tiles** view, then click on the **Arrange** option which is present on the right-hand side of the library.

5. Now, you can see all your library columns as shown in the following screenshot:

Compact list

In a list view each item will be shows with a grey color border for each row, but in compact list it removes that, it just showed the items in a compact view(without additional space between each item)

1. Like the **Tiles** view, **Compact list** is also a new feature of the modern SharePoint library where you can see your documents in the compact form.

2. To create this **Compact list** view, go to the **All Documents** option which is present at the top right corner page of the document library. Then, click on the **Compact list** option from the drop-down menu.

3. After creating the compact list, the documents will be seen as shown in the following screenshot:

Select Documents and Download in a .zip Format

1. Another new feature of the modern SharePoint document library is **download as a Zip**. This **Download as a Zip** option helps to download single or multiple documents in the .zip format.

2. To download the documents from the document library, select all the documents that are present in the document library and then click on the **Download** option which is present at the top of the library. Then, the document will be ready to open the .zip files:

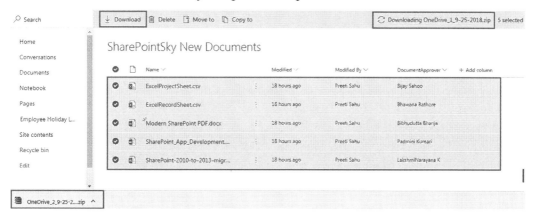

Share the Documents with Others

1. The modern SharePoint library provides another feature which is the **Share** option. This **Share** option is used to share the details of a document from one person/user to another person or another user.

2. To share the document details, just select the SharePoint document and then go to the **Share** option which is present at the top of the library and on the right-hand side of the selected document as shown in the following screenshot:

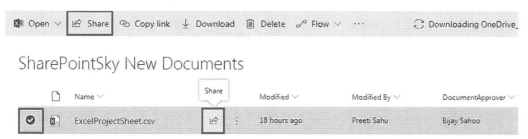

3. Enter a username which specifies to whom you want to send the document link. So, the link can be edited by that specific user only. Also, you can send the document link to multiple users at a time.

4. You can also give some **Subject Line** about the document which is present under the **User** field. Then, click on the **Send** option to send the document:

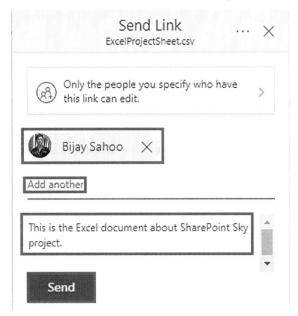

5. After clicking on the **Send** option, a message that the document link is sent to another user will be displayed as shown in the following screenshot:

Copy Link and Outlook Options

1. These are the two basic features which are provided by the modern SharePoint libraries/list. The **Copy Link** and **Outlook** options are present in the **Share** feature of the modern SharePoint document library which I have discussed above.

2. While sharing the files/documents from one person to another person, you can see the **Copy Link** and **Outlook** options in the **Send Links** page as shown in the following screenshot:

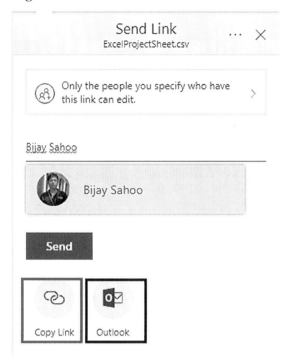

3. If you click on **Copy Link** (highlighted in red), you will see a copied status of the selected document as shown in the following screenshot. This means your selected document link is copied.

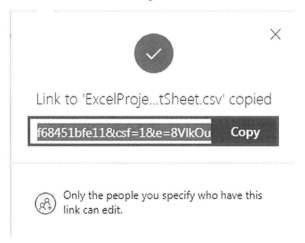

4. If you click on **Outlook** (highlighted in black), you will see a **Creating Shareable link...** status of the selected document as shown in the following screenshot:

Stop Document Sharing

1. **Stop sharing** is a new feature of the modern SharePoint library/list which was not available in the classic SharePoint library/list.

2. If you want to stop sharing any document to any user, then select the document and click on the **Share** option which is present on the right-hand side of the selected document and at the top of the modern SharePoint library:

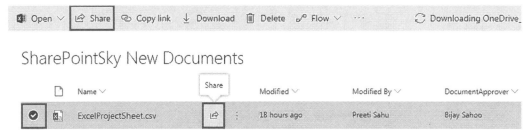

3. Then, the **Send Link** page appears on the screen in the existing library page only. On this page, you can see the "**...**" option which is present at the top of the page. Just click on this ... option and then click on the **Manage Access** option as shown in the following screenshot:

4. Now, the **Manage Access** page appears on the right-hand side of the document library. On this page, you will see all the user names with whom you can share the list items. Here, you can give the user permissions to anyone by using the **Grant Access** option which is present at the top of the page.

5. If you want to stop sharing an item, which means it will disable all the links giving access to this item and remove all people with direct access except the owners, then click on the **Stop sharing** option as shown in the following screenshot:

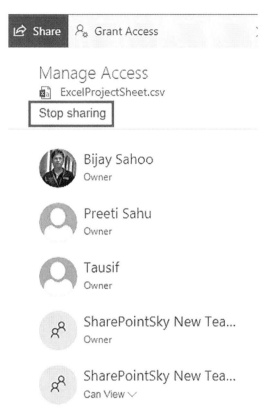

6. When you click on the **Stop sharing** option, it will disable all links and remove all people with access except owners:

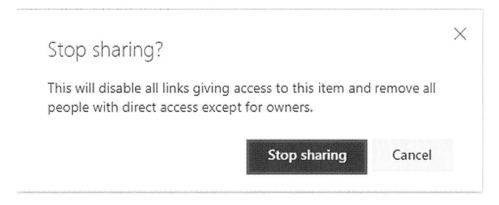

Move to Selected Documents from One Site to Another Site

Move to is a new feature which is present in the modern SharePoint Online document library. If you want to move a document from one site collection to another site collection or any other document library, you can use the **Move to** option.

Let's take a look at the following example:

1. Here, in the following screenshot, I want to move the document, ExcelRecordSheet.csv, from this document library to any other site of the document library. To do this, I need to select the document and then click on the **...** option which is present at the top of the library. Then, I need to click on the **Move to** option:

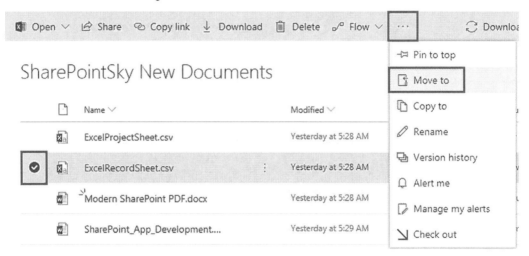

2. After clicking on the **Move to** option, the **Places** page appears on the right-hand side of the existing library page where I need to choose the place where I need to move the document. The **Places** page populates all the site collections from your Office 365 tenant. Here, I have chosen the **TSInfo Technologies** site as shown in the following screenshot:

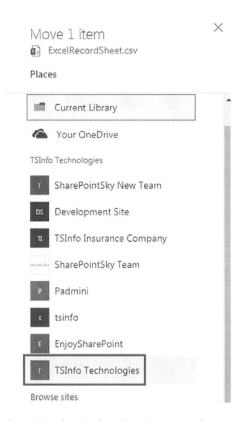

3. After choosing the **TSInfo Technologies** site, the **Destination Page** will be displayed. Here, you need to choose the destination where you want to move that document. Basically, the page will show all the document libraries. Here, I have selected the Documents folder as shown in the following screenshot:

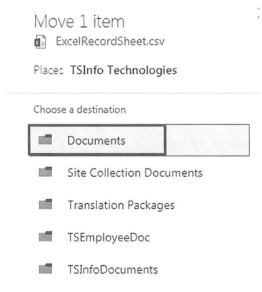

4. After choosing the destination as Documents, it will ask you to create a New folder where the document will be moved. So, you need to click on New folder to create a new folder in another site:

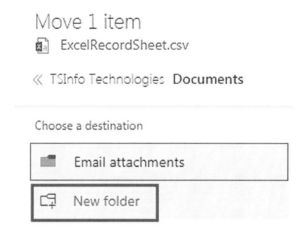

5. Then, you need to give a name to the New folder. I have named it ExcelRecord as shown in the following screenshot. Now, just click on the **Move here** option:

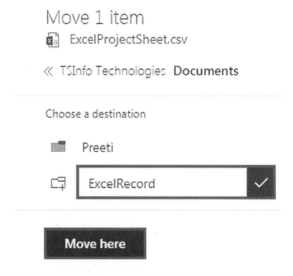

6. Now, if you go to the destination site where you moved the document, you will be able to see the Document folder named ExcelRecord as shown in the following screenshot:

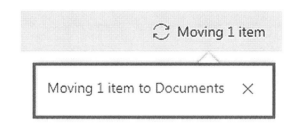

Copy to Selected Documents from One Site to Another Site

1. In the same way, you can copy the selected document from the current site to another site or any other document library. So, **Copy to** is a new feature of modern SharePoint Online which is provided by Microsoft. As the same process of **Move to** feature, you can do the **Copy to**" feature process.

2. To copy one document, just select the particular document and click on the **Copy to** feature option which is present at the top of the library. Then, follow the same steps as in the **Move to** feature:

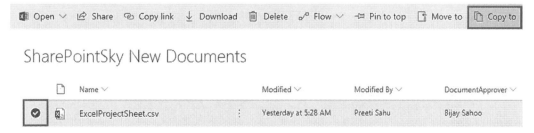

3. Here also, you need to select the destination where you want to copy the document. It can be any other site collections or any other document library:

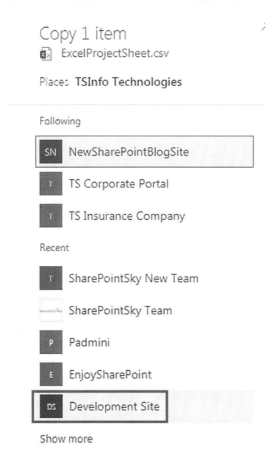

Note: It will display destination site based on the user permission. You can only copy or move documents to sites which you have permissions to. If user does not have permission, then the site will not appear.

And if Meta data are missing in the destination document library then it will ignore the Meta data for the document library. But it will copy the document.

Select and Bulk Edit properties

1. **Bulk edit properties** is purely a new feature of the modern SharePoint Online document library which helps to edit the bulk amount of document value at a time.

2. To edit the value of every column at a time, you can use **Bulk edit properties**. Go to the Document Details Pane which is present at the top right corner of the document library. Here, you can see the **Bulk edit properties** feature.

3. Enter the username in the **DocumentApprover** column which will affect all the documents of document library. Click on **Save**.

4. Now, in the following screenshot, you can see the username (**Bijay Sahoo**) in the **DocumentApprover** column is affected by using the **Bulk edit properties** feature:

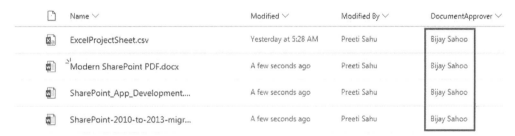

Create Microsoft Flow

As you know, Microsoft Flow is in full demand for business automation tasks. You can directly create a flow from the modern SharePoint Online document library as shown here:

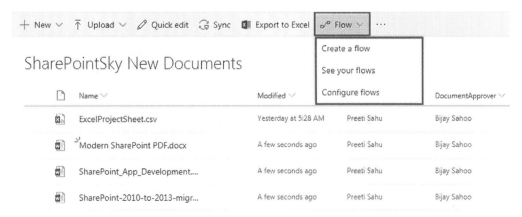

Just click on the **Create a flow** button to create a flow for the document library. If you are new to Microsoft flow, you can read a detailed article on Microsoft Flow.

Pin to Top of Each Document

1. **Pin to top** is a new feature of the modern SharePoint library which helps to pin the important documents at the top. So the user can easily recognize his/ her important documents.

2. To insert or place the important document at top of the library as **Pin to top**, select a particular document which you want to pin to the top. Then, go to the **Pin to top** option which is present at the top of the library as shown in the following screenshot:

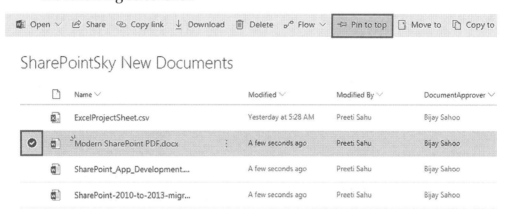

3. In the following screenshot, you can see that the Modern SharePoint PDF. docx document is now at the top by using the **Pin to top** feature:

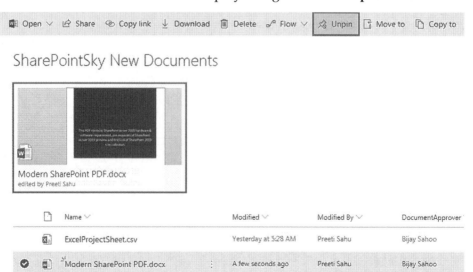

4. If you want to unpin the particular document, then select the **Pin to top** document and click on the **Unpin** option which is present at the top of the document library. Then, your document will unpin.

Export to Excel

1. In the classic SharePoint Online document library, the **Export to Excel** feature was working only one browser i.e. Internet Explorer which supports **ActiveX**.

2. But in the modern SharePoint Online document library, the **Export to Excel** feature works in various browsers such as Chrome, Firefox and so on.

3. **The Export to Excel** feature is normally present at the top of the document library as shown in the following screenshot. By using this feature, we can export the document to Excel:

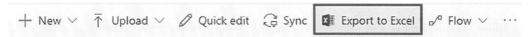

4. When you open the Excel file, you will see the documents in an Excel sheet as shown in the following screenshot:

Alert Me Notification

1. The modern SharePoint library/list provides the **Alert me** feature which is already present in the classic SharePoint library/list with an old look.

2. When someone changes any file, folder or any document in your document library, you get an alert or notification that your files or documents are changed by someone.

3. You can find the **Alert me** option at the top of the document library as shown in the following screenshot:

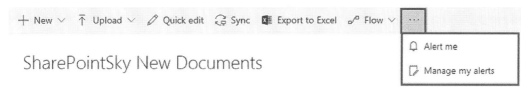

Order the Library Column as Ascending or Descending

1. Order is a feature of the modern SharePoint document library where you can change the order depending on your existing column. The two types of orders in the order feature are as follows:

   - **A to Z** (ascending order)

   - **Z to A** (descending order)

2. Click on the library column which you want to keep in proper order and then select the **A to Z** (ascending) order option from that drop-down column.

3. You can see that specific column in a proper ascending order in the following screenshot:

Mandatory Field Validation Notification

1. The modern SharePoint document library created the latest mandatory field validation notification feature which will be very useful to the user. Let's take a look at the following example.

2. Here, I have created a column by using the **+ Add column** option which is the **Choice** column as shown in the following screenshot:

3. After clicking on the **Choice** option, the **Create a column** page appears on the existing library page where you need to enter the details of a column such as:

- **Name**: Single line of text which should be a mandatory field
- **Description**: Multiline of text
- **Type**: **Choice**
- **Choices**: **Approved/Pending** as per your requirement

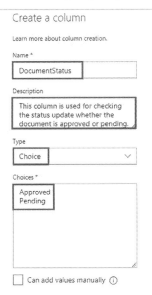

4. Then, set the **Default value** as **None**. In **More options**, select **Drop-Down Menu** under **Display choices using** and also enable the **Require that this column contains information** option. Then, click on the **Save** option to save the details of the library column:

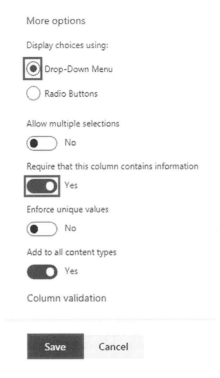

5. Now, the new choice column named DocumentStatus is created. In the following screenshot, I did not fill the choice column. Therefore, the **Required info** notification appears in this column. That's why a yellow mark mandatory field validation appears on the right-hand side of the library.

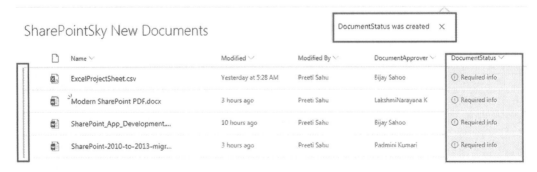

6. To fill the information in the DocumentStatus choice column, just click on the **Required info** tab as shown in the following screenshot:

7. Then, the settings pane will be displayed on the right-hand side of the library page where you need to enter the column details of the particular document.

8. Then, go to the DocumentStatus column and select the **Approved/Pending** option from the dropdown as per your requirement. Then, it will be saved automatically in the list.

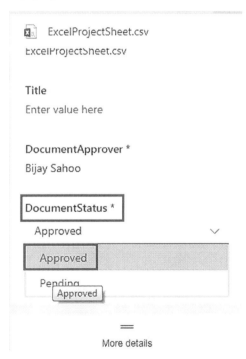

9. In the following screenshot, you can see that the yellow mark validation has vanished in the choice columns where I have entered the data and the yellow mark validation still shows in the columns where the data has not been entered. If you fill the choice columns of all documents, then the yellow mark validation will not be displayed any further:

SharePointSky New Documents

	Name ∨	Modified ∨	Modified By ∨	DocumentApprover ∨	DocumentStatus ∨
	ExcelProjectSheet.csv	About a minute ago	Preeti Sahu	Bijay Sahoo	Approved
	Modern SharePoint PDF.docx	A few seconds ago	Preeti Sahu	LakshmiNarayana K	Pending
	SharePoint_App_Development....	10 hours ago	Preeti Sahu	Bijay Sahoo	ⓘ Required info
	SharePoint-2010-to-2013-migr...	4 hours ago	Preeti Sahu	Padmini Kumari	ⓘ Required info

Filter by Column

1. **Filter by** is another new feature in the modern SharePoint library which is used to filter the column value.

2. To filter the value of a column, click on a specific column which you want to filter and then click on the **Filter by** option from the drop-down column as shown in the following screenshot:

SharePointSky New Documents

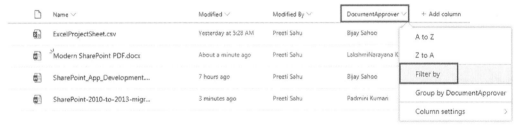

3. Then. the Filter by column (Name of your Column) page appears on the right-hand side of your existing library page where you need to give the filter value of whatever you want to filter as shown in the following screenshot:

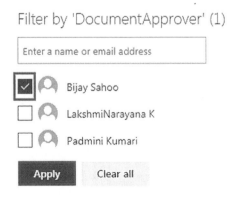

4. Now, you need to select a specific type which you want to filter either a **Word** file or **CSV** file as shown in the following screenshot. You can see the result of that specific date filter value.

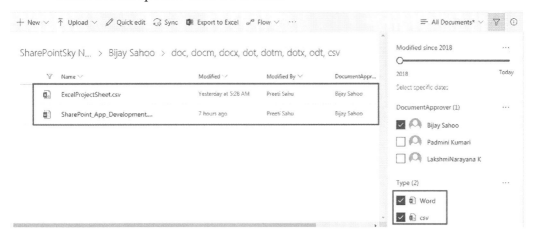

Group by the Column

1. The modern SharePoint document library provides a new feature, **Group by**. Previously, it was not present in the classic SharePoint document library.

2. If you want to group items or documents by any library column, go to that particular library column and click on the **Group by** with the specific column name from the drop-down column as shown in the following screenshot:

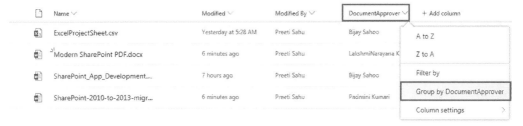

3. You can see the **Group by** (with that specific column name) feature in the following screenshot:

SharePointSky New Documents

		Name ∨	Modified ∨	Modified By ∨	DocumentAppr... ∨
∧					
∧		DocumentApprover: Bijay Sahoo (2)			
		ExcelProjectSheet.csv	Yesterday at 5:28 AM	Preeti Sahu	Bijay Sahoo
		SharePoint_App_Development....	7 hours ago	Preeti Sahu	Bijay Sahoo
∧		DocumentApprover: LakshmiNarayana K (1)			
		Modern SharePoint PDF.docx	8 minutes ago	Preeti Sahu	LakshmiNarayana K
∧		DocumentApprover: Padmini Kumari (1)			
		SharePoint-2010-to-2013-migr...	9 minutes ago	Preeti Sahu	Padmini Kumari

Save View as in the Modern SharePoint Document Library

1. **Save view as** is a new feature with a new look which is provided by the modern SharePoint document library.

2. To see the result of the **Save view as** option, first change something in your library column. For example, here I have changed the order of the title column **A to Z** as shown in the following screenshot:

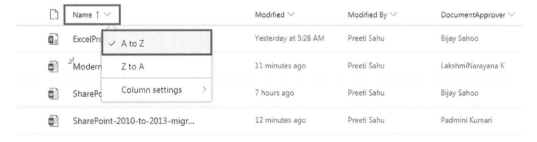

SharePointSky New Documents

	Name ↑ ∨		Modified ∨	Modified By ∨	DocumentApprover ∨
	ExcelPr	✓ A to Z	Yesterday at 5:28 AM	Preeti Sahu	Bijay Sahoo
	Modern	Z to A	11 minutes ago	Preeti Sahu	LakshmiNarayana K
	SharePo	Column settings >	7 hours ago	Preeti Sahu	Bijay Sahoo
	SharePoint-2010-to-2013-migr...		12 minutes ago	Preeti Sahu	Padmini Kumari

3. Now, go to the **All Documents*** option which is present at the top right corner of the modern SharePoint document library. Then, click on the **Save view as** option to save changes or to create a new view as shown in the following screenshot:

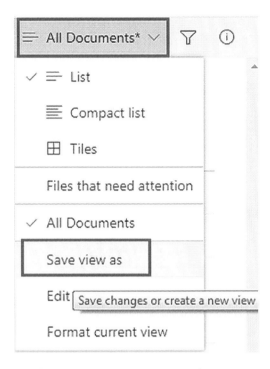

4. After clicking on the **Save view as** option, the **Save as** page appears on the same page where you need to type a new name to save the current view. Check the checkbox of the **Make this a public view** option and click on **Save** to save the new view.

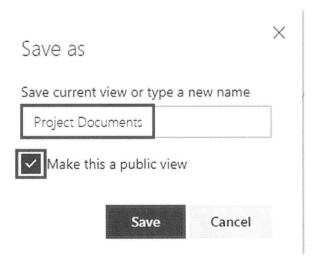

5. Once the view is saved, you can see the current view **Project Documents** which is saved as shown in the following screenshot:

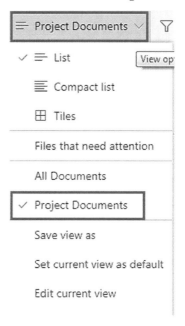

Edit View Columns

1. **Edit view columns** is purely a new feature which is present in the modern SharePoint document library which helps you to select the columns to be displayed in the list view.

2. Go to any one of the library columns. Click on **Column settings** and then click on the **Show/hide columns** option.

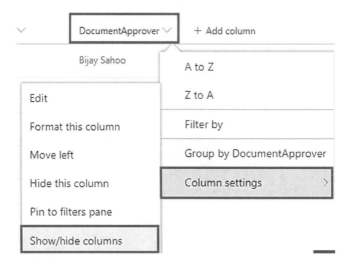

3. When you click on the **Show/hide columns** option, the **Edit view columns** page appears on the right-hand side of the library page.

4. If you want to display any columns in the list view, select the columns you want.

5. Similarly, if you want to change the order of the column, you can use drag and drop or up and down buttons as shown in the following screenshot:

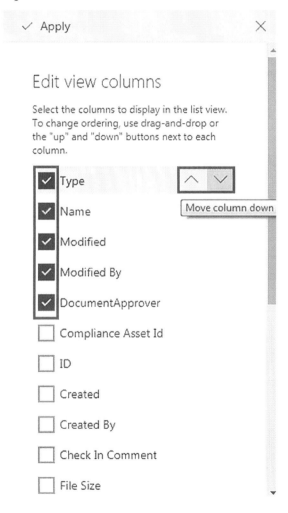

6. Here, I have changed the order of columns by using the drag and drop option and then clicked on the **Apply** option. The order of columns have changed as shown in the following screenshot:

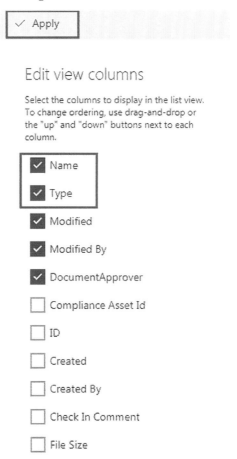

Open the ECB Menu just on a right click

1. The new feature in the modern SharePoint document library defines that when you right click on any place in the document library, the ECB menu opens directly.

2. When a user wants to open the ECB menu, there is no need to go to any option. By right clicking, it will directly open the library page as shown in the following screenshot:

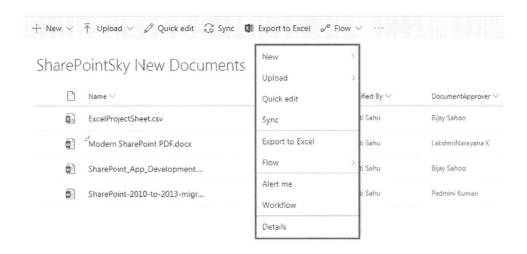

Files That Need Attention

1. A new feature released by Microsoft is **Files that need attention** which is present in the modern SharePoint document library. We are familiar with the necessary metadata and sometimes we forget to assign the metadata. We can use the attention view to resolve this.

2. If you forget to give any value to the column field, a mandatory field validation notification appears in the document library as shown in the following screenshot.

3. To keep with your attention of any document with mandatory field values, go to the **All Documents*** option which is present at the top of the library. Then, click on the **Files that need attention** feature:

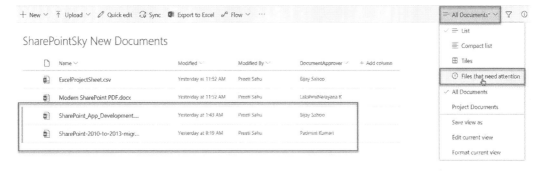

4. After clicking on the **Files that need attention** feature, you will able to see the **Missing info** column as shown here:

5. To resolve this **Missing info** column, click on the specific document of **DocumentStatus missing** and then in the document pane, directly go to that missing column and edit the value as per your requirement and it will be saved automatically.

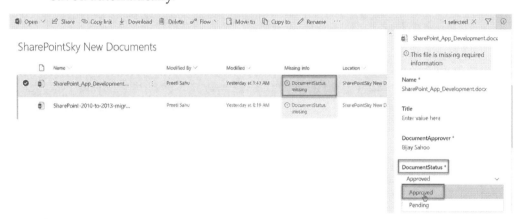

6. After saving the column field value, the **Missing info** will change to **Resolved** as shown in the following screenshot:

Edit New Menu

Edit New menu is a new feature of the document library which helps to edit/modify some new menu of the library:

1. To go to the **Edit New menu** option, click on the **+ New** drop-down menu. Then, select the **Edit New menu** option as shown in the following screenshot:

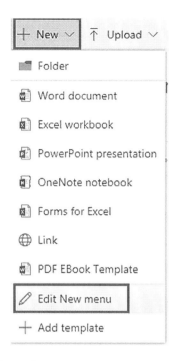

2. When you click on the **Edit New menu** option, the edit settings page appears on the existing page as shown in the following screenshot.

3. If you don't want to view some options in the **+ New** option, then uncheck those options on the **Edit New menu** settings page and click on **Save**.

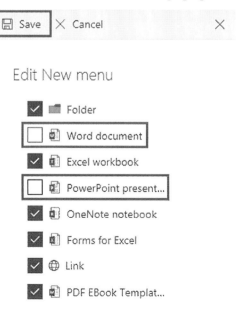

4. Now, go to the **+ New** option in the document library. Here, you can see that the unchecked options are not available in the drop-down menu as shown in the following screenshot:

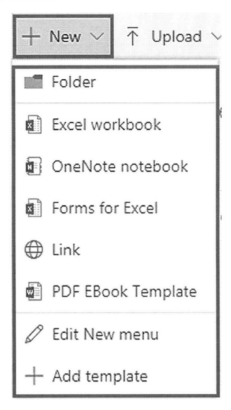

Move up and Move down Options of the Edit New Menu

The **Edit New menu** option in the modern library feature has the following two properties:

- Move up
- Move down

1. If you want to view the menu in up, then go to the vertical ellipses option of a particular menu, select the **Move up** option and then click on **Save** as shown in the following screenshot:

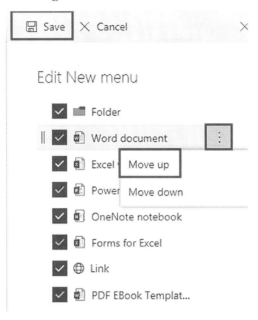

2. After clicking on the **Move up** option, go to the **+ New** option in the modern document library. Here, you can see that the selected menu has already been moved upward as shown in the following screenshot:

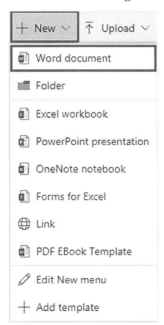

3. If you want to view the menu in down, then go to the vertical ellipses option of a particular menu, select the **Move down** option and then click on **Save** as shown in the following screenshot:

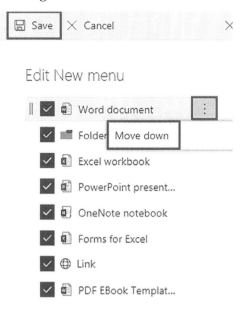

4. After clicking on the **Move down** option, go to the **+ New** option in the modern document library. Here, you can see that the selected menu has already been moved downward as shown in the following screenshot:

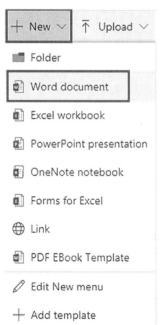

Add Templates

Microsoft has added a new feature known as **+ Add template** in the modern document library.

1. With the help of this new feature, you can add a new template to the **+ New** drop-down option and you can directly use the template by clicking on it once.

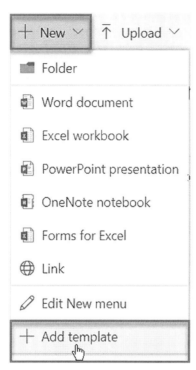

2. When you click on the **+ Add template** feature, it will ask you to add the template you want. To add the template, the browsing page will display the location from where you can get your template easily as shown in the following screenshot:

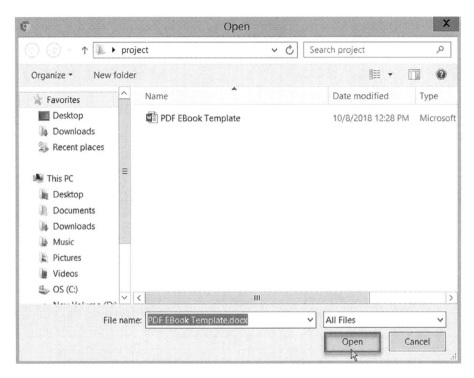

3. After adding the new template, go to the **+ New** drop-down option in the modern document library. Here, you can view your new template in the menu. So, by clicking on the new template once, you can use your new template.

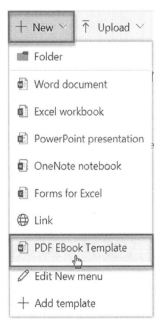

SharePoint Online Modern List and Library Column Customization / Formatting Using JSON

Column customization/formatting using JSON is the latest feature of the modern SharePoint list and library released by Microsoft and can be added easily. Column customization/formatting is nothing but a display of SharePoint lists/library columns with proper formatting. This means you can show your data/record in a designing manner. To do this, you can use JSON code in the existing list/library column as per your requirement.

The following two lists with the **Due Date**, **Assigned To**, **Effort(Days)** fields from the **Employee Task** list and the **Product Brand**, **Sales Status** field from the **Sales Marketing** list customized via column formatting might look like this:

Employee Task

Task Name ∨	Due Date ∨	Assigned To ∨	Action ∨	Effort(Days) ↑ ∨
Designer Workflow	11/20/2018	Preeti Sahu ✉	⟲ Send to Manager	1
Modern SharePoint	11/22/2018	Bijay Sahoo ✉	⟲ Send to Manager	2
Nintex Workflow	11/20/2018	LakshmiNarayana K ✉	⟲ Send to Manager	3
SharePoint Framework	11/19/2018	Bibhudutta Bhanja ✉	⟲ Send to Manager	5
Microsoft Flow	11/26/2018	Padmini Kumari ✉	⟲ Send to Manager	6

Sales Marketing

Product Brand ∨	Product Name ∨	Sales Performed ∨	Sales Target ∨	Sales Status ∨
BMW	BMW MOTORRAD	7,000	7,000	✓ Done
AUDI	AUDI FREIRAUM	7,000	8,000	→ In Progress
MERCEDES-BENZ	MERCEDES-BENZ MAYBACH	11,000	12,000	ⓘ In review
FORD	FORD ECOSPORT	4,000	6,000	⚠ Has Issues
TOYOTA	TOYOTA LUXURY	1,000	6,500	⊘ Blocked

Formatting an Item When a Date Column is Before or After Today's Date

You can format or customize the date column before or after today's date. You can simply say the date is overdue. The above example colors the current field red when the value inside an item's **Due Date** is before the current date.

So for this date customization, create a list and also create a column such as **Due Date** as per your requirement:

To add the JSON code to the **Due Date** column, click on the drop-down icon of the **Due Date** column and then click on **Column settings** and **Format this column** as shown in the following screenshot:

After clicking on **Format this column**, a text box appears on the existing page where you need to add the JSON code for date formatting. Click on the **Save** button.

If you want to preview this JSON code, then click on **Preview** and view the list. The JSON code is as follows:

```
{
  "$schema": "https://developer.microsoft.com/json-schemas/sp/column-
    formatting.schema.json",
  "elmType": "div",
  "debugMode": true,
  "txtContent": "@currentField",
  "style": {
    "color": "=if([$DueDate] <= @now, '#ff0000', ''"
  }
}
```

Format column   >

Change the display of this column by adding JSON below. Remove the text from the box to clear the custom formatting.

Learn more about formatting columns with JSON

```
{
   "$schema":
"https://developer.microsoft.com/json-
schemas/sp/column-
formatting.schema.json",
   "elmType": "div",
   "debugMode": true,
   "txtContent": "@currentField",
   "style": {
     "color": "=if([$DueDate] <= @now,
'#ff0000', ''"
   }
}
```

Preview   Save   Cancel

After adding the JSON code, you can view your list items. In the following screenshot, you can see that the **Due Date** turns red in color because of an overdue problem:

Employee Task

Task Name ∨	Due Date ∨
Designer Workflow	11/20/2018
Modern SharePoint	11/22/2018
Nintex Workflow	11/20/2018
SharePoint Framework	11/19/2018
Microsoft Flow	11/26/2018

Add an Action Button to a Field for Sending an Email

You can use column formatting to add an action link next to the fields. This means by clicking on an action button, you can open a mailbox and send an email to another person.

If you are creating a custom list, make sure your list column is **Person**. Then, only it will work.

The following example illustrates the **Person** field column, i.e., **Assigned To**. So, you need to add an action button code to this field only:

EmployeeTask

| Completed ∨ | Task Name ∨ | Due Date ∨ | Assigned To ∨ |

To add the JSON code to the **Assigned To** column, click on the drop-down icon of the **Assigned To** column and then click on **Column settings** and **Format this column** as shown in the following screenshot:

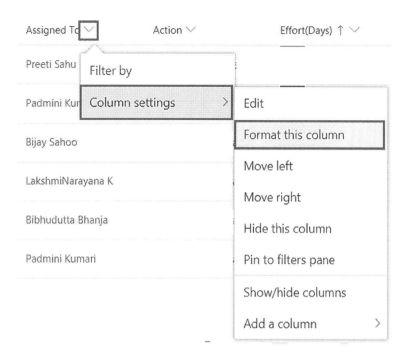

After clicking on **Format this column**, a text box appears on the existing page where you need to add the JSON code to add an action button to send an email. Then, click on the **Save** button.

If you want to preview this JSON code, then click on **Preview** and view the list. The JSON code is as follows:

```
{
  "$schema": "https://developer.microsoft.com/json-schemas/sp/column-
    formatting.schema.json",
  "elmType": "div",
  "children": [
   {
     "elmType": "span",
     "style": {
       "padding-right": "8px"
     },
     "txtContent": "@currentField.title"
   },
   {
     "elmType": "a",
```

```
   "attributes": {
     "iconName": "Mail",
     "class": "sp-field-quickActions",
     "href": {
       "operator": "+",
       "operands": [
         "mailto:",
         "@currentField.email",
"?subject=Task status&body=Hey, how is your task coming along?.\r\n---\r\n",
         "@currentField.title",
         "[$ID]"
       ]
     }
    }
   }
  ]
}
```

Format column   ×

Change the display of this column by adding JSON below. Remove the text from the box to clear the custom formatting.

Learn more about formatting columns with JSON

```
{
  "$schema":
"https://developer.microsoft.com/json
-schemas/sp/column-
formatting.schema.json",
  "elmType": "div",
  "children": [
    {
      "elmType": "span",
      "style": {
        "padding-right": "8px"
      },
      "txtContent":
"@currentField.title"
    },
    {
      "elmType": "a",
      "attributes": {
```

Preview   Save   Cancel

Once you save the JSON code, the **Assigned To** column appears with the mailbox icon as shown in the following screenshot:

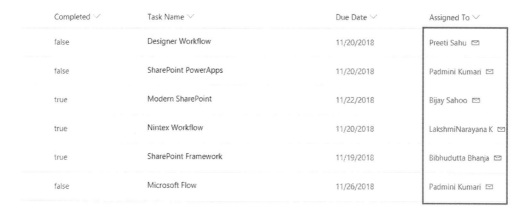

When you click on the mailbox icon, Outlook directly opens as shown here. By using this mailbox icon, you can easily send emails to anyone without navigating to the other page:

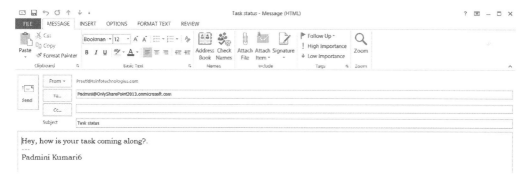

Create a Button to Launch a Flow

By using the JSON code, you can create a button to launch the flow. So for this flow button formatting, create a column such as **Action** as per your requirement.

To add the JSON code to the **Action** column, follow the given steps:

1. Click on the drop-down icon of the **Action** column and then click on **Column settings** and **Format this column** as shown in the following screenshot:

2. After clicking on **Format this column**, a text box appears on the existing page where you need to add the JSON code to create a button to launch the flow. Then, click on the **Save** button.

3. If you want to preview this JSON code, then click on **Preview** and view the list. The JSON code is as follows:

```
{
 "$schema": "https://developer.microsoft.com/json-schemas/sp/column-
          formatting.schema.json",
 "elmType": "span",
 "style": {
  "color": "#0078d7"
 },
 "children": [
  {
```

```
    "elmType": "span",
    "attributes": {
      "iconName": "Flow"
    }
  },
  {
    "elmType": "button",
    "style": {
      "border": "none",
      "background-color": "transparent",
      "color": "#0078d7",
      "cursor": "pointer"
    },
    "txtContent": "Send to Manager",
    "customRowAction": {
      "action": "executeFlow",
      "actionParams": "{\"id\": \"1ae295d2-acae-483f-95c7-4ff086bf0295\"}"
    }
  }
  ]
}
```

In the preceding code, the id must be your Microsoft Flow ID in the actionparams method.

To obtain the Microsoft Flow ID, follow the given steps:

1. Choose flow and see your flows in the SharePoint list where the flow is configured.

2. Choose the flow you want to run.

3. Copy the ID from the end of the URL.

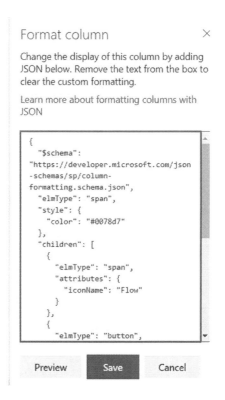

Once you save the JSON code, the **Action** column appears with the flow icon and the text content will be **Send to Manager** (as it has been added to the text content in the code) as shown in following screenshot.

Once you click on the **Send to Manager** action, it will directly open Microsoft flow. By clicking on this flow icon, you can easily view the flow without navigating to the other page:

Employee Task

Task Name ∨	Due Date ∨	Assigned To ∨	Action ∨
Designer Workflow	11/20/2018	Preeti Sahu ✉	⚙ Send to Manager
Modern SharePoint	11/22/2018	Bijay Sahoo ✉	⚙ Send to Manager
Nintex Workflow	11/20/2018	LakshmiNarayana K ✉	⚙ Send to Manager
SharePoint Framework	11/19/2018	Bibhudutta Bhanja ✉	⚙ Send to Manager
Microsoft Flow	11/26/2018	Padmini Kumari ✉	⚙ Send to Manager

Format a Number Column as a Data Bar

Formatting a number column as a data bar helps to create a data bar visualization of a column which should be a **Number** column of a SharePoint list/library.

To create this data bar visualization, follow the given steps:

1. Create a column field which should be a **Number** column. In the following screenshot, **Effort(Days)** is a number column:

2. To add the JSON code to the **Effort(Days)** column, click on the drop-down icon of the column and then click on **Column settings** and **Format this column** as shown in the following screenshot:

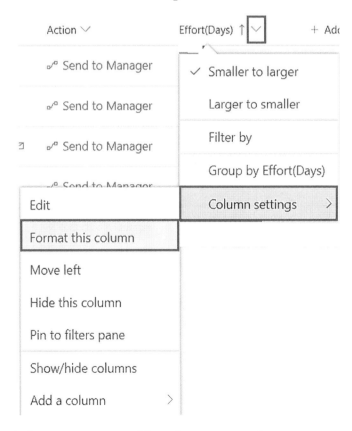

3. After clicking on **Format this column**, a text box appears on the existing page where you need to add the JSON code to design the number column as data bar. Then, click on the **Save** button.

4. If you want to preview this JSON code, then click on **Preview** and view the list. The JSON code is as follows:

```
{
"$schema": "https://developer.microsoft.com/json-schemas/sp/column-
          formatting.schema.json",
"elmType": "div",
"txtContent": "@currentField",
"attributes": {
  "class": "sp-field-dataBars"
},
"style": {
  "width": "=if(@currentField> 95, '100%', toString(@currentField * 100 / 95) +
          '%'"
  }
}
```

Format column   〉

Change the display of this column by adding JSON below. Remove the text from the box to clear the custom formatting.

Learn more about formatting columns with JSON

```
{
  "$schema":
"https://developer.microsoft.com/json-
schemas/sp/column-
formatting.schema.json",
  "elmType": "div",
  "txtContent": "@currentField",
  "attributes": {
    "class": "sp-field-dataBars"
  },
  "style": {
    "width": "=if(@currentField > 25,
'50%', toString(@currentField * 100 /
10) + '%'"
  }
}
```

Preview   Save   Cancel

5. Once you save the JSON code, the **Effort(Days)** column appears with the data bar as shown in the following screenshot:

Employee Task

Completed ∨	Task Name ∨	Due Date ∨	Assigned To ∨	Action ∨	Effort(Days) ↑ ∨
false	Designer Workflow	11/20/2018	Preeti Sahu ✉	✎ Send to Manager	1
true	Modern SharePoint	11/22/2018	Bijay Sahoo ✉	✎ Send to Manager	2
true	Nintex Workflow	11/20/2018	LakshmiNarayana K ✉	✎ Send to Manager	3
true	SharePoint Framework	11/19/2018	Bibhudutta Bhanja ✉	✎ Send to Manager	5
false	Microsoft Flow	11/26/2018	Padmini Kumari ✉	✎ Send to Manager	6

Create Clickable Actions Which Turn Field Values into Hyperlinks

You can create a clickable hyperlink action that provides hyperlinks that can go to the other webpages. You cannot use column formatting to output links to protocols other than http://, https://, or mailto://.

To create the clickable action hyperlinks, follow the given steps:

1. Choose a column field from the modern SharePoint list. In the following screenshot, **Product Brand** is a single line of text column:

Sales Marketing

Product Brand ∨	Product Name ∨	Sales Performed ∨	Sales Target ∨

2. To add the JSON code to the **Product Brand** column, click on the drop-down icon of this column and then click on **Column settings** and **Format this column** as shown in the following screenshot:

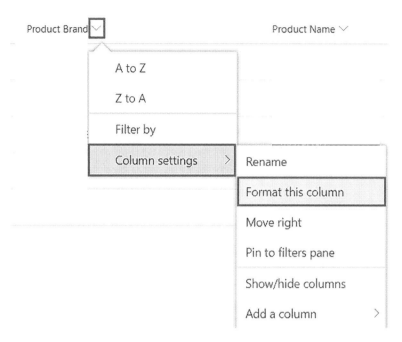

3. After clicking on **Format this column**, a text box will appear on the existing page where you need to add the JSON code to create a clickable hyperlink action. Then, click on the **Save** button.

4. If you want to preview this JSON Code, then click on **Preview** and view the list. The JSON code is as follows:

```
{
    "$schema": "https://developer.microsoft.com/json-schemas/sp/column-
            formatting.schema.json",
    "elmType": "a",
    "txtContent": "@currentField",
    "attributes": {
        "target": "_blank",
        "href": "='http://finance.yahoo.com/quote/' + @currentField"
    }
    "style": {
        "color": "='#ff0000', ''"
    }
}
```

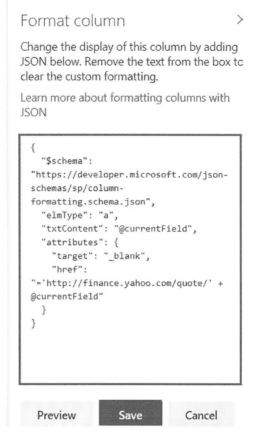

5. Once you save the JSON code, the **Product Brand** column appears with the hyperlink references as shown in the following screenshot:

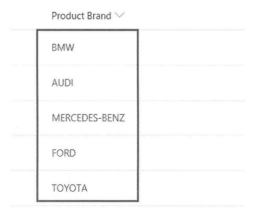

Quickly How to Change the Background and Text Color of a Column

We can create a column formatting where you can see quickly how to change the background and text color of a column.

To create this column formatting, follow the given steps:

1. Choose a column field from the modern SharePoint list. In the following screenshot, **Product Name** is a single line of text column:

2. To add the JSON code to the **Product Name** column, click on the drop-down icon of this column and then click on **Column settings** and **Format this column** as shown in the following screenshot:

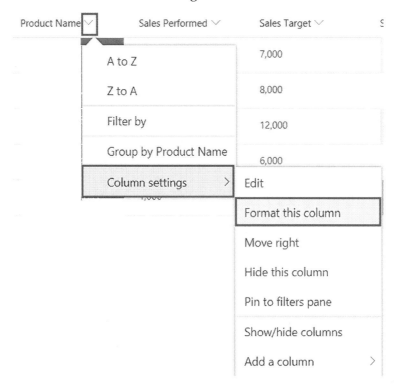

3. After clicking on **Format this column**, a text box will appear on the existing page where you need to add the JSON code to change the background and text color. Then, click on the **Save** button.

4. If you want to preview this JSON Code, then click on **Preview** and view the list. The JSON code is as follows:

```
{
    "$schema": "http://columnformatting.sharepointpnp.com/
            columnFormattingSchema.json",
    "debugMode": true,
    "elmType": "div",
    "txtContent": "@currentField",
    "style": {
            "background-color": "#2E8B57",
            "color": "lightblue",
            "padding-left": "10px"
    }
}
```

Format column   >

Change the display of this column by adding JSON below. Remove the text from the box to clear the custom formatting.

Learn more about formatting columns with JSON

```
{
    "$schema":
"http://columnformatting.sharepointpnp.
com/columnFormattingSchema.json",
    "debugMode": true,
    "elmType": "div",
    "txtContent": "@currentField",
    "style": {
        "background-color": "#2E8B57",
        "color": "lightblue",
        "padding-left": "10px"
    }
}
```

Preview   Save   Cancel

5. Once you save the JSON code, the **Product Name** column appears with the background color and the text color as shown in the following screenshot:

Conditional Formatting Based on the Value in a Text or Choice Field

This conditional formatting feature is based on the value in a text or choice field. This formatting helps to map different values to different levels of urgency.

The following example applies different classes depending on whether the field value is **Done**, In **Review**, **Blocked**, **Has issues**, **In Progress** and so on.

To create this conditional formatting, follow the given steps:

1. Choose a column field from the modern SharePoint list which is text or choice column. In the following screenshot, **Sales Status** is a choice column:

2. To add the JSON code to the **Sales Status** column, click on the drop-down icon of this column and then click on **Column settings** and **Format this column** as shown in the following screenshot:

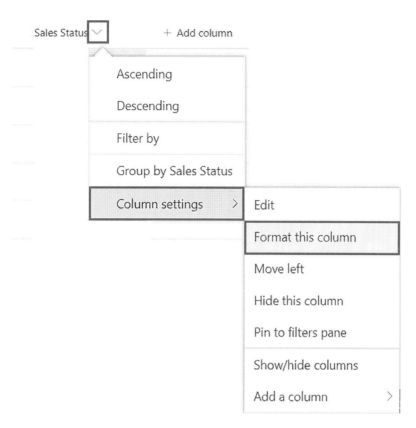

3. After clicking on **Format this column**, a text box will appear on the existing page where you need to add the JSON code for conditional formatting. Then, click on the **Save** button.

4. If you want to preview this JSON code, then click on **Preview** and view the list. The JSON code is as follows:

```
{
"$schema": "https://developer.microsoft.com/json-schemas/sp/column-
       formatting.schema.json",
"debugMode": true,
"elmType": "div",
"attributes": {
  "class": "=if(@currentField == 'Done', 'sp-field-severity--good', if(@currentField
       == 'In Progress', 'sp-field-severity--low' ,if(@currentField == 'In
       review','sp-field-severity--warning', if(@currentField == 'Blocked','sp-
       field-severity--blocked', ''))"
},
"children": [
```

```
{
  "elmType": "span",
  "style": {
    "display": "inline-block",
    "padding": "0 4px"
  },
  "attributes": {
    "iconName": "=if(@currentField == 'Done','CheckMark', if(@currentField
        == 'In Progress', 'Forward', if(@currentField == 'In review', 'Error',
        if(@currentField == 'Has Issues','Warning', if(@currentField
        =='Blocked','blocked','')))"
  }
},
{
  "elmType": "span",
  "txtContent": "@currentField"
}
]
}
```

Format column   ×

Change the display of this column by adding
JSON below. Remove the text from the box to
clear the custom formatting.

Learn more about formatting columns with
JSON

```
{
  "$schema":
"https://developer.microsoft.com/json
-schemas/sp/column-
formatting.schema.json",
  "debugMode": true,
  "elmType": "div",
  "attributes": {
    "class": "=if(@currentField ==
'Done', 'sp-field-severity--good',
if(@currentField == 'In Progress',
'sp-field-severity--low'
,if(@currentField == 'In review','sp-
field-severity--warning',
if(@currentField == 'Blocked','sp-
field-severity--blocked', ''))"
  },
  "children": [
```

Preview   Save   Cancel

5. Once you save the JSON code, the **Sales Status** column appears with the field value as in the conditional-based icon with the background color as shown in the following screenshot:

Sales Marketing

Product Brand ∨	Product Name ∨	Sales Performed ∨	Sales Target ∨	Sales Status ∨
BMW	BMW MOTORRAD	7,000	7,000	✓ Done
AUDI	AUDI FREIRAUM	7,000	8,000	→ In Progress
MERCEDES-BENZ	MERCEDES-BENZ MAYBACH	11,000	12,000	⊙ In review
FORD	FORD ECOSPORT	4,000	6,000	⚠ Has Issues
TOYOTA	TOYOTA LUXURY	1,000	6,500	⊘ Blocked

Summary

In this chapter, we learned about the features of SharePoint Online in detail. We learned about the **Site contents** and **Add an app** options, the settings page and document details pane and learned how to manipulate the width of the column and **Alert me** notification. We also took a look at the list and library customization/formatting using JSON. In the next chapter, we will take a look at the section layouts, properties of section layouts, and web parts of the SharePoint Online modern team site.

CHAPTER 6

SharePoint Online Modern Site Pages

Microsoft has released a new era with big changes in Modern SharePoint Online i.e. *modern site page*. This is one of the best updated features in the modern SharePoint Online which is very fast and easy to author.

In this modern site page, the pages look very attractive on any device in a browser. These pages contain various types of web parts which you can customize depending on your requirements. In modern pages, the **SharePoint Framework (SPFx)** web part can be added easily. Some of the web parts are given here which we can use in SharePoint modern pages:

- Text
- Image
- File Viewer
- Link
- Highlighted contents
- Embed
- Events

Creating Modern SharePoint Site Pages

You can create modern SharePoint Site pages using the following two ways:

- Using the **Site contents** option
- Using the left navigation bar

Create a Site page Using Site contents

1. Go to the Gear icon which is present at the top of the modern home page. Then, click on the **Site contents** option as shown here:

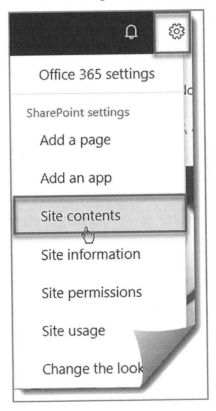

2. On the **Site contents** page, click on the **Site Page** option:

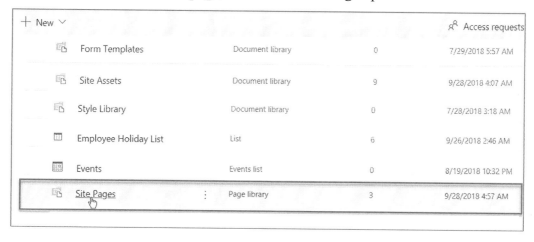

3. After clicking on **Site Pages**, click on the **+ New** option and choose the **Site Page** option from the drop-down menu to create a modern SharePoint site page:

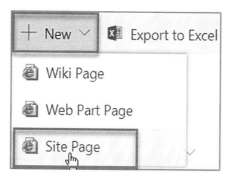

4. The following screenshot displays the attractive look of a modern SharePoint site page:

Using the Left Navigation Bar

1. Another easy way to create a Site **Page** is by using the left navigation bar of your modern home page. Just click on the **Pages** option of left navigation as shown here:

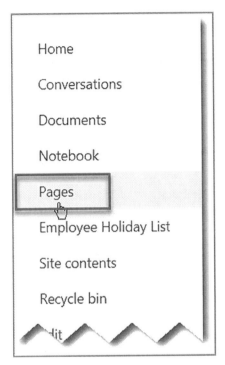

2. In the **Site Page** option, click on the **+ New** option which is present at the top of the page. Choose **Site Page** from the drop-down menu:

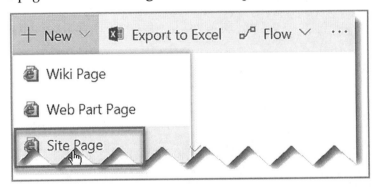

3. Then, it displays a modern site page which looks attractive as shown in the following screenshot:

What is a SharePoint Online Modern Site Page?

Recently, Microsoft team released SharePoint Online modern site pages which look great on any device, in a browser, etc. Modern SharePoint Online site pages are faster than classic SharePoint Online site pages.

Sometimes, in the classic SharePoint site, while you will try to add Site page for designing, then the Site Page option will not come. For this, you need to activate the **Site Page** feature under the **Manage Site Feature**. Once you activate this feature, you can see the **Site Page** option from the drop-down menu.

Modern SharePoint site pages consist of some web parts, which you can design according to your requirements. You can just select the + option and add a web part easily from the toolbox to add the content to your page.

Designing of a Site Page

You can design your modern site page by using the various options such as page title, change the image of page, remove the image of page, etc. Also, you can customize the site page by using different types of modern web parts.

The modern SharePoint Online site pages are responsive in nature.

Here are the following options to design a modern site page:

1. **Page Title**: As shown in the following screenshot, you can give your site page a title by using the **Name your page** option:

2. **Change image**: Similarly, if you want to change the image of the site page, then by using the **Change image** option you can change the image:

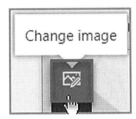

3. When you click on **Change image**, it will ask you to choose an image from the various options as follows:

- **Recent**: This shows your recently uploaded images.

- **Web search**: If you want to search an image from any website, then this option will help you to choose the image.

- **Site**: If you want to choose the image from any site, then the **Site** option will help you to choose the image.

- **Upload**: If you want to upload an image from your PC, then this option will help you upload the image.

- **From a link**: If you want to choose an image from a particular link, then this option will help you to do so.

4. **Remove image**: If you don't want to keep the site page image or if you want to keep a new image, then you can remove the site page image by using the **Remove image** option as shown in the following screenshot:

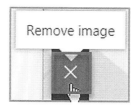

5. **Reset to default image**: You can reset the site page image by using the **Reset to default image** option. When you click on this option, it will reset the default image:

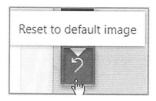

The Modern SharePoint Online Site Pages Tabs

The modern site page tabs have the following four important options:

1. **Save and close**: This **Save and close** option helps to save the modern site page you have designed and then closes the site page.

2. **Discard changes**: This **Discard changes** option helps to remove all the changes you had made earlier in the modern site page:

3. **Page details**: If you want to view the details of modern site pages, then click on **Page details** from the tab. Then, it will show you the modern site page details as shown in the following screenshot:

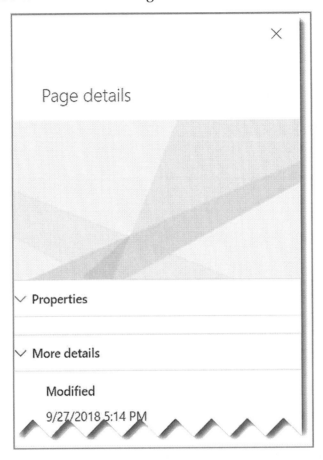

4. **Publish**: Once the modern site page is designed, click on the **Publish** option which helps to publish the site page for a better look.

Set a Custom Site Page as a Home Page

You can customize your modern site page as a home page. That is, if you have designed an attractive modern site page and you want to customize the site page as the home page, then you can set this site page by following the given steps:

1. Go to the **Site Page** option which is present at the **Site contents** page and as well as on the left navigation bar.

2. On the **Site Page**, select the modern site page that you want to set as your home page. Then, go to the **...** symbol which is present at the top of the page and select **Make homepage:**

3. After selecting the **Make homepage** option, you can view your modern site page as the home page as shown in the following screenshot:

Add a Custom Site Page to the Navigation

Navigation is a helpful thing that helps to the user to search the SharePoint contents easily. In the navigation bar, by clicking one link only, the user can get his/her contents.

To add the custom site page to navigation, follow the given steps:

1. Go to the **Site Page** option and select your modern site page that you want to add to navigation.

2. Then, click on the **Add to navigation** option which is present at the top of the page as shown in the following screenshot:

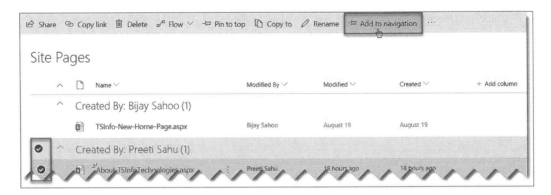

3. Then, the modern site page will appear in the left navigation as shown here:

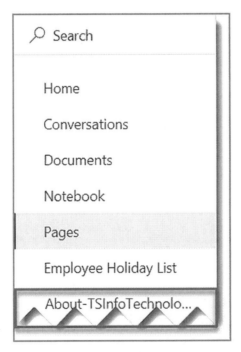

New Modern SharePoint Online Site Page's Section Layout

At the time of writing this book, there are five different types of modern page layouts are present. To add the new section layout to the modern site page, click on the + symbol which is present at the left edge of the page and then choose your new layouts as shown in the following screenshot:

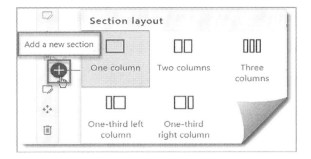

The five different types of new section layouts are as follows:

1. **One column**: If you choose the section layout as **One column**, the layout appears in one column in the modern site page as shown in the following screenshot:

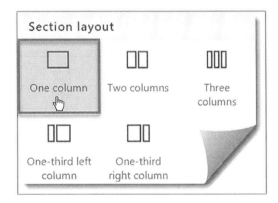

2. **Two columns**: If you choose the section layout as **Two columns**, the layout appears in two columns in the modern site page as shown in the following screenshot:

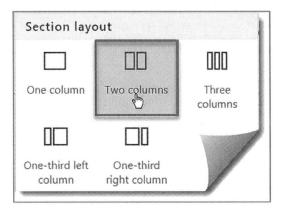

3. **Three columns**: If you choose the section layout as **Three columns**, the layout appears in three columns in the modern site page as shown in the following screenshot:

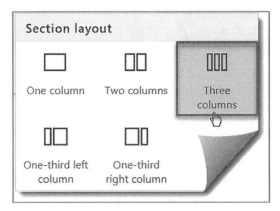

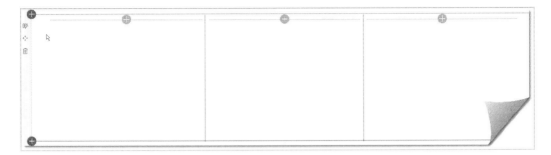

4. **One-third left column**: If you choose the section layout as **One-third left column**, the layout appears in one-third left column in the modern site page as shown in the following screenshot:

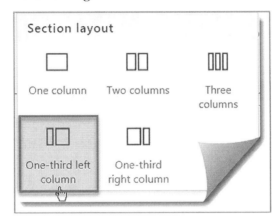

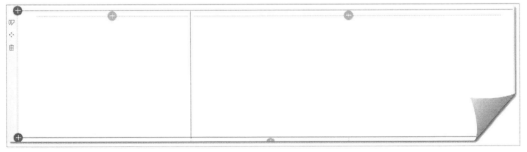

5. **One-third right column**: If you choose the section layout as **One-third right column**, the layout appears in one-third right column in the modern site page as shown in following screenshot:

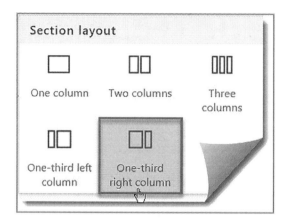

Properties of the New Section Layout

There are three new properties that are present vertically at each section layout in the modern site pages. They are as follows:

- **Edit section**: This option helps to edit the section.

- **Move section**: This option helps to move the section from one section layout to another section layout within the modern site page.

- **Delete section**: This option helps to remove/delete the section layout.

Add Web Parts to a SharePoint Online Modern Site Page

What are Modern SharePoint Web Parts?

Microsoft has released built-in apps which are nothing but modern SharePoint web parts which help to process various types of content. For example, to store a document, there is a web part (app) which is called 'Document Library'; similarly, the 'Calendar' web helps to store an event of an organization, and the 'Weather' web part helps to know about the weather information or weather temperature and so on.

In the previous sections, we discussed new section layouts. Now, we need to create the new web parts. By using these new web parts, a user can design an attractive page.

Follow the given steps to add web parts to the SharePoint Online modern site page:

1. To create a new web part, click on the + option which is present in each and every section layout.

2. After clicking on this option, a web part box appears on the screen in the existing modern site page.

3. In this web part box, you can view different types of web parts as shown in the following screenshot. Microsoft also provides a search box in the web part box so that a user can easily get a web part according to their requirements:

4. If you want to see all the web parts at a time, just click on the maximize arrow as shown in the following screenshot:

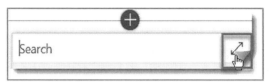

5. Once you maximize the arrow mark, it will show you all categories (types) of web parts as follows:

- **Featured**: This contains **Text, Image, File viewer** and so on.

- **Text, media, and content**: This contains **Bing maps, Divider, Embed** and so on.

- **Discovery**: This contains **Document library (preview), Hero, Highlighted content, List** and so on.

- **Communication and collaboration**: This contains **Events, Group calendar, Microsoft Forms** and so on.

6. In the **Featured** category, you cannot see all the web parts at a time. So to see all the web parts, click on the **See all** option which is present on the right-hand side of the page as shown in the following screenshot:

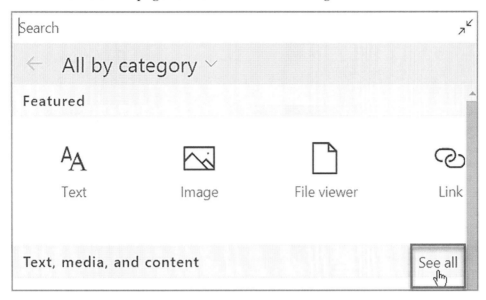

7. When you click on the **See all** option, you can see the remaining web parts as shown in the following screenshot:

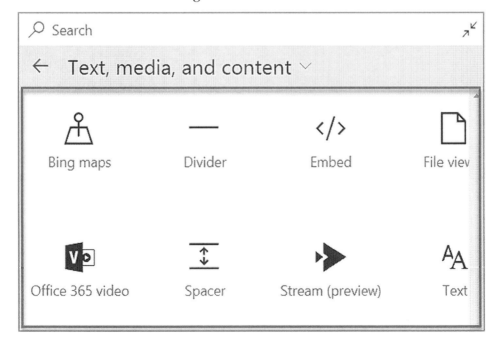

Summary

In this chapter, we learned about the features of the modern SharePoint Online and how to create the site pages using the **Site content** option and left navigation bar. We also learned about the section layouts and how to add web parts to our site pages. In the next chapter, we will take a look at the web parts in detail.

CHAPTER 7

Explorer SharePoint Online Modern Experience Web Parts

Microsoft has released several modern web parts which help to make site pages load faster. Web parts are building blocks for your site pages in SharePoint. Web parts help to make your page more attractive. You can add text, images, lists, libraries, links, etc. to your page as web parts. You can customize web parts as per your needs.

We have different out of box web parts available in SharePoint Online modern sites. Following are the out of box web parts that can be added to a page.

Text

The **Text** web part allows you to type text or paragraph. To add text web part, follow the given steps.

1. To add the **Text** web part, click on the + option and then click on **Text**:

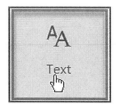

2. When you click on the **Text** web part, a text box appears on the screen where you can type any text, paragraph, etc. as shown in the following screenshot:

3. You can also provide an attractive look to the text by using some designer properties as mentioned below:

- **Normal text/font style**: If you want to choose a font and size for the text, then click on the **Normal text** drop-down menu. You can choose **Heading 1** or **Heading 2,** and soon.

- **Bold**: By using this option, you can make the text bold or highlight it.

- **Italic**: By using this option, you can change the text font to an italic font style.

- **Underline**: If you want to underline some words, then you can choose this option.

- **Alignment**: This option is used to align the text to the right, left, or center according to your design.

- **Bulleted list**: If you have any list in the text box, then by using this option, you can use bullet points.

- **Hyperlink**: If you want to add hyperlinks to any word or any sentence from the text, you can do so by using this option:

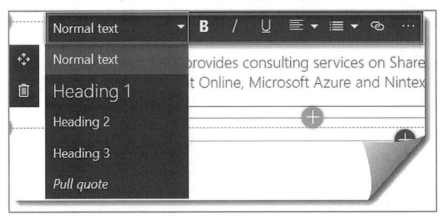

- At the extreme end of the formatting bar, the **...** icon is present which allows the user to view more options. Now, click on this option:

- Once you click on this option, it will show you the remaining properties of the text field box like **Undo**, **Redo**, **Font size**, **Insert table**, and so on:

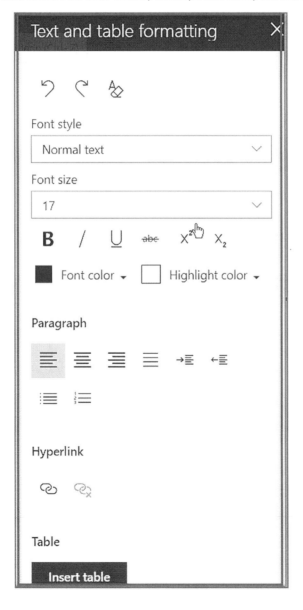

Move and delete Text web part

You can move the **Text** web part from one layout to another layout in the modern page. If you want to move the web part, then click on the Move web part icon as shown in the following screenshot:

If you want to remove/delete the **Text** web part, then click on the delete icon and it will remove the web part from the modern site page.

Image

The **Image** web part allows you to insert different types of images in the modern site page. To add Image web part, follow the given steps.

1. To add the **Image** web part, click on the **+** option and then click on **Image**:

2. When you click on the **Image** web part, the following screen appears. To add the image, click on the **Add image** button:

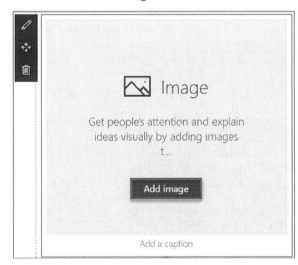

3. When you click on the **Add image** option, it will ask you to insert the image from different options like **Recent**, **Web search**, **OneDrive**, **Site**, **Upload**, **From a link**. Then, choose the specific option from where you want to insert the image and then click on **Add item** to add the image:

4. After adding the image, it will appear as shown in the following screenshot. You can also add a caption in the image web part. Similarly, you can edit, move and also delete this web part:

File viewer

The **File viewer** web part allows you to view your all files/folders/documents in the modern site page. To add the File Viewer web part, follow the steps given below:

1. To add the **File viewer** web part, click on the + option and then click on **File viewer**:

2. When you click on the **File viewer** web part, it will ask you to choose your files/folders/documents that you want to view in the **File viewer** web part. So, you can choose your files from various options such as **Recent**, **OneDrive**, and so on:

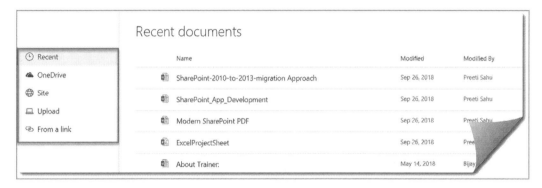

3. On successful uploading of the file/folder/document, it will appear as shown in the following screenshot. Here, you can give a 'caption' for the file view:

Link

The **Link** web part helps you to display any image, video or any text by using only the hyperlink URL. To add the Link web part, follow the given steps:

1. To add the **Link** web part, click on the + option and then click on **Link**:

2. When you click on the **Link** web part, a blank link box appears on the screen. Now, you need to provide a hyperlink URL at the top of this web part after which it will appear on the screen as shown in the following screenshot:

Embed

By using only the embed code or website address, you can see any videos, images, etc. So, for this option, there is a web part in the modern site page named **Embed**. By using this web part, you can directly insert the code and play a video. The steps to add this web part are given below:

1. To add the **Embed** web part, click on the + option and then click on **Embed** or you can easily find the web part by typing in the search box:

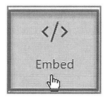

2. When you click on the **Embed** web part, the embed box appears on the screen where you can insert your embed code/website address as shown in the following screenshot:

3. Now, the video will appear in that particular web part and you can play that video as shown in the following screenshot; you can also give a subject line to the video:

Highlighted content

If you have any important documents/files/folders, you can highlight them in your modern site page using the **Highlighted content** web part. To add this web part, follow the given steps:

1. To add the **Highlighted content** web part, click on the **+** option and then click on **Highlighted content** or you can easily find this web part by typing in the search box:

2. When you click on **Highlighted content**, the screen will directly show you the recent documents you have used. Here, you can also give the titke of the highlighted content as shown in the following screenshot:

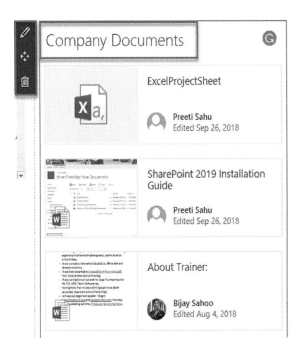

Bing maps

The **Bing maps** web part helps to show the exact location of a specific place like any company, any residential area, etc. By giving a particular address, it will show you the exact place. To add this web part, follow the given steps:

1. Click on the **+** option and then click on the **Bing maps** web part. You can easily find the web part by typing in the search box:

2. When you click on **Bing maps**, a location map appears on the screen where you need to search your specific location by using the search box. It will show you the map location of that place as shown in the following screenshot; you can also give a location title:

Properties

Below are few properties of Bing Maps

1. **Change map image background:** If you hover your mouse over the **Road** option, it will ask you to choose any background image from the drop-down menu. After choosing the background, it will show you the updated image background:

2. **Zoom in and Zoom out map location:** To view the location as per your choice, you can zoom in and zoom out the map by using the **+** (zoom in) and **-** (zoom out) options:

Divider

Divider is a web part which divides/separates two things at a time. To add this web part, follow the given steps:

3. To add the **Divider** web part, click on the **+** option and then click on **Divider**. You can easily find the web part by typing in the search box:

4. Then, you will see a **Divider** icon appear on your existing modern site page as shown in the following screenshot:

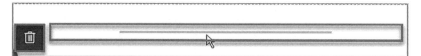

Document library (preview)

The **Document library (preview)** web part helps you to view only one of the document libraries from all the documents that are present in your existing SharePoint site. To add the web part, follow the given steps: Note: At the time of writing this book, it was still in preview, but now you may find like "Document library".

1. If you want to view your document library in the modern SharePoint site page, then add the **Document library (preview)** web part by using the search box:

2. When you click on the **Document library (preview)** web part, a **Document library** dialog box appears on the screen where you need to select a document library that needs to be added to the modern site page as shown in the following screenshot:

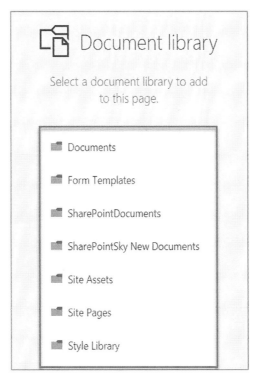

3. After selecting your specific document library from the dialog box, the modern site page will look as shown in the following screenshot:

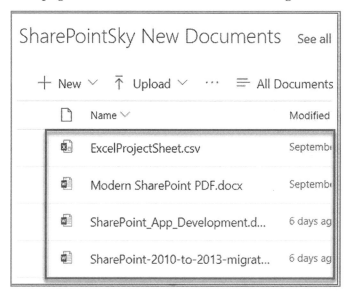

By using this **Document library** web part, you can upload a new document, delete your existing document, save as view, and so on. All these things you can modify in the site page only. By using the modern site page you can do all the things whatever you are doing in the Document library such as adding a new document, uploading a document, and so on.

Events

The Events web part helps you to show all the events of an organization where people can see it. When you add an event, the **Events** web part helps to show the event where your readers can see it. To add the web part, follow the given steps:

1. To add the **Events** web part, click on the + option and then click on **Events**. You can easily find this web part by typing in the search box:

2. When you click on the **Events** web part, a screen appears as shown in the following screenshot. To add the latest events, click on the **+ Add event** or **Create an event** link. Make sure that the page is in the publish mode so that you can add the events in the publishing mode. You can also give your event a name at the top of the web part:

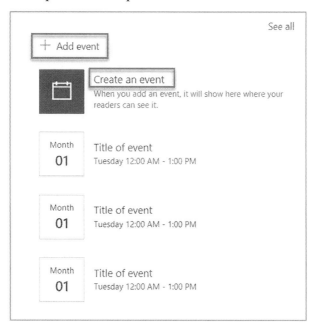

3. When you click on the **+Add event** option, an event site page appears on the screen where you need to provide the details of events as follows:

   - **Event title**: You can give the title of the event.

   - **When**: This option helps to choose the date from the calendar and also choose the timing of that event.

   - **Where**: In this option, you need to enter a specific location where the event is organized.

   - **Link**: In this option, you need to enter an online meeting link as well as the display name of the event.

   - **Category**: In this option, you need to select a category like meeting, business, anniversary, etc. from the drop-down menu.

   - **About this event**: In this option, you can add some text or paragraph about the event. You can also design this text/paragraph by using the various properties like bold, italic, font size, etc.

   - **Name or email address**: In this option, you need to specify the user who will join the Event by using their name or email address.

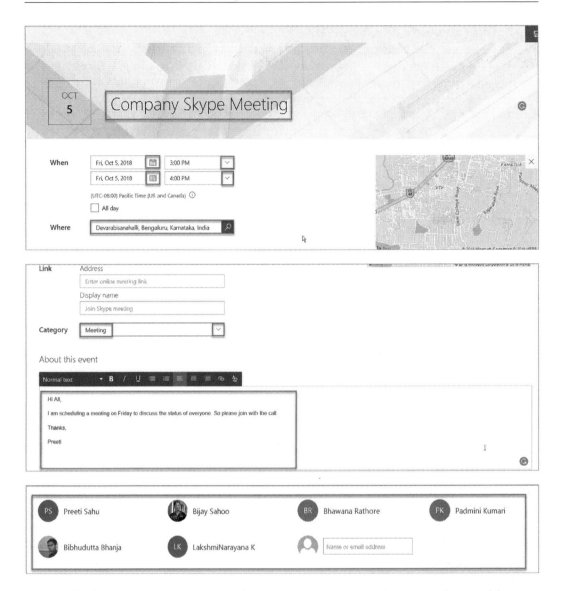

4. In the same way, you can add one or more events by using the **+Add event** option. If you want to see all the events of the web part, then click on the **See all** option which is present at the top of the web part:

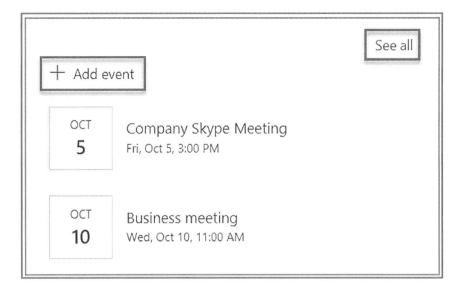

5. When you click on the **See all** option, you can view all the events as shown in the following screenshot:

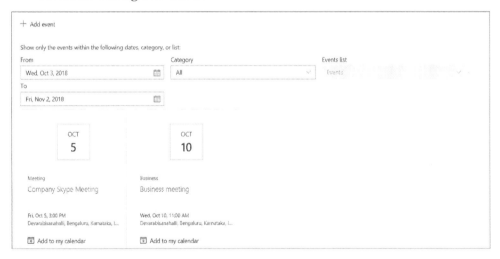

GitHub

Microsoft provides **GitHub** web part which has a connector associated to connect to GitHub. This GitHub connector sends notifications about activities related to your GitHub projects. To add this web part, follow the given steps:

1. To add the **GitHub** web part, click on the **+** option and then click on **GitHub**. You can easily find this web part by typing in the search box:

2. When you click on the **GitHub** web part, you will be asked to sign in to your GitHub account to add the connector as shown in the following screenshot:

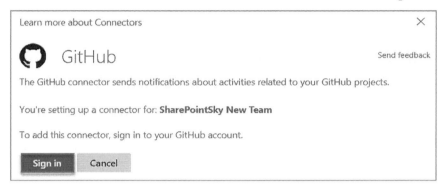

3. Once the sign in is completed, it will show you the **Authorize Microsoft Office 365 Connectors** screen. Click on the **Authorize connmgt** button as shown in the following screenshot:

4. After authorization, you will be asked to choose the GitHub account you want to use to set up the connector or add a new account. To create a new account, click on **Add a new GitHub account**.

5. Select a GitHub repository from the drop-down menu that can be configured. Also, check the notifications as per your needs and then click on the **Save** button as shown in the following screenshot:

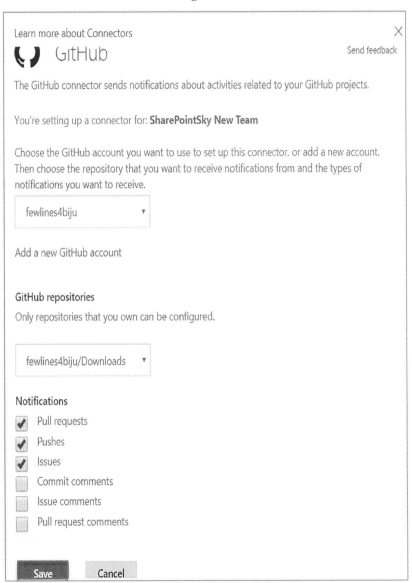

6. Once you save the GitHub connector, the GitHub web part will be displayed on the modern site page as shown here:

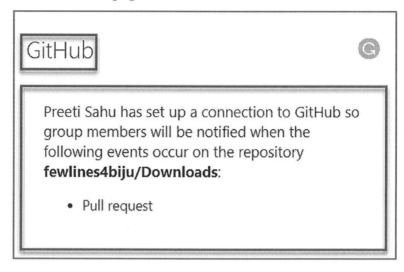

Hero

Note: Before we add the **Hero** web part, make sure that you choose the **Section layout** option as **One column** or **One-third right column**, or else the edit page will not appear due to its small size layout. And if you select the **One-third left** layout, then add the **Hero** web part in the second half.

We can add the **Hero** web part to a modern SharePoint online site home page by following the given steps:

1. Click on the + option and then click on the **Hero** web part. You can easily find this web part by typing in the search box:

2. When we add the **Hero** web part, it displays the screen as shown in the following screenshot. Then, go to the **Edit** mode of the **Hero** web part. Here, the **Layout** option will come to choose the **Hero** layout. There are two layout options: **Tiles** and **Layers**.

3. First, select the **Tiles** layout and here you can choose any tiles you want. I have chosen **Five tiles** so the tiles appear in the five-tiles layout as shown in the given screenshot:

4. Here, if you select the **Layers** option and then select **Two layers**, the page will be displayed in two layers:

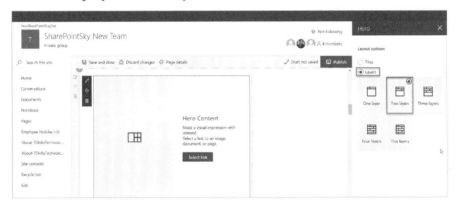

5. I chose the **Tiles** option so the screen looks like as shown in the following screenshot. Now, click on the **Select link** button of the **Hero** web part:

6. When you click on **Select link**, an upload item page appears on the screen for uploading the image. You can upload the image by using various options like **Recent, Web search, OneDrive, Site, Upload,** and **From a link**.

7. Here, I have selected the **Upload** option to upload the image from my system. Then, I clicked on **Add item** to add the image:

8. Go to the **Edit** mode of the first section of the **Hero** web part. The settings page appears on the existing site. Here, you can see the **Link** option. If you want to show a specific website from the internet, then you can change the URL. Just click on the **Change** button:

9. As I need the URL address from a link, I need to click on the **From a link** option, copy the website address from the internet and paste the link in the box. Then, I need to click on the **Open** option:

10. Now, the URL link has changed in the **Hero Settings** page. Here, you can also give the title. I have given the title **SharePoint** as shown in the following screenshot. If you want to show the title in the layout, enable the **Show title in layout** option:

11. In the **Image** option, select **Custom image** and if you want to change the image, then click on the **Change** option and change the image of the **Hero** web part. You can also give the **Alternative text**, which the people cannot see.

12. If you want to show the call to the action link, then enable the **Show call to action link** option:

13. Similarly, you can fill the remaining section layouts. After filling all the sections of the **Hero** web part, you can see the whole structure of the **Hero** web part as shown in the following screenshot:

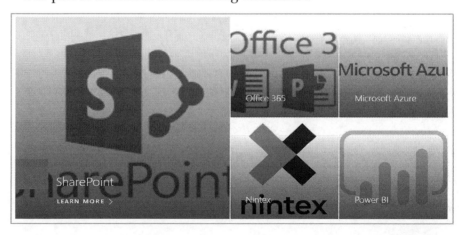

Image gallery

The **Image gallery** web part helps you to make a gallery of images like company images, any team member images, any company project images, etc. Follow the given steps to add the **Image gallery** web part:

1. To add the **Image gallery** web part, click on the **+** option and then click on the **Image gallery** web part. You can easily find this web part by typing in the search box:

2. When you click on the **Image gallery** web part, the following screen appears. You need to add the images by clicking on the **+ Add** option or the **Add images** button:

3. You can add the image by using various options like **Recent, OneDrive, Site, Upload**, etc. After choosing your image from these options, just click on **Add image** to add the image to the **Image gallery** web part:

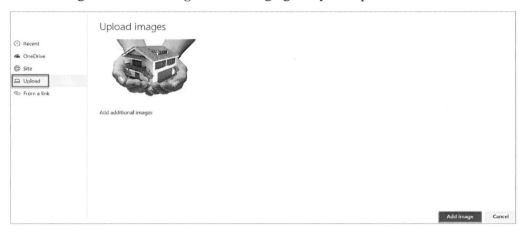

4. Now, you can see your image as shown in the following screenshot. You can also directly give an image title in the web part. To know more about the image, go to the **Edit** mode of that image:

5. In the **Edit** mode, an **Image gallery** setting page appears on the screen where you need to enter the **Title, Caption, Alternative Text** of the image. People will be able see the title and caption of the image when they view this image as shown in the following screenshot:

6. You can add a number of images of your choice to the image gallery by using the **+Add** option:

7. If you want to add any extra design in the **Image gallery** web part, go to the **Edit** mode of the **Image gallery** web part. The **Image gallery** setting page appears on the existing page.

8. On the setting page, you can see **Image options** in the drop-down menu. Under **Image options**, you need to select any one of the options. If you want to select the image in the same site, then choose the **Select images** option. Then, the images will appear as shown below:

9. If you want to dynamically display images from a document library, select the **Dynamically display images from a document library** option. You can select a particular document from the drop-down document library.

10. You need to choose the maximum number of images to be displayed from the **Maximum number of images to display** drop-down menu.

11. The three layouts in the **Image gallery** web part are as follows:

• **Tiles**: If you click on the **Tiles** layout, then the **Image gallery** web part will look like as shown in the following screenshot. If you want to give the ratio, then choose any aspect ratio from the drop-down menu:

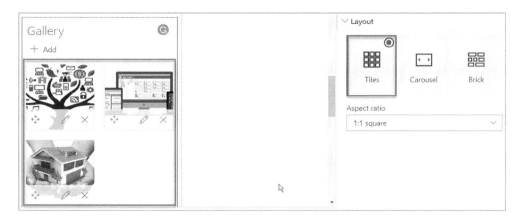

- **Carousel**: If you click on the **Carousel** layout, then the **Image gallery** web part will be displayed like a slide show. You can enable or disable the **Automatically cycle through images** option. If you want to give the timing between each change of images, then drag the **Seconds between each change of images** slider:

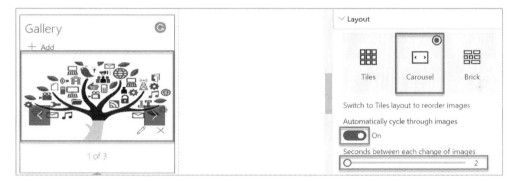

- **Brick**: If you click on the **Brick** layout, the **Image gallery** web part will look like a brick as shown in the given screenshot:

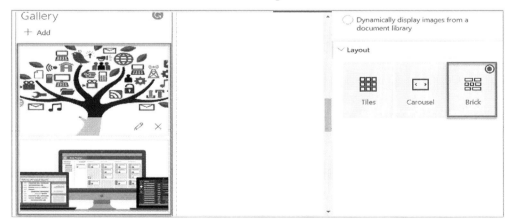

JIRA

JIRA is a tool which is used for bug tracking, issue tracking, and project management activities

SharePoint provides the **JIRA** web part which helps you to send notifications about the activities related to your team. You can communicate with JIRA tool from this JIRA web part from SharePoint sites.

To use the JIRA connector, you'll need to create certain settings on the JIRA website by following a few easy steps. If you don't have an account, then create one on the **JIRA** website. To add this web part, follow the given steps:

1. To add the **JIRA** connector web part, click on the + option and then click on **JIRA**:

2. When you click on the **JIRA** web part, you need to enter a name for your JIRA connection. Then, click on the **Create** button to create a new JIRA account as shown in the following screenshot:

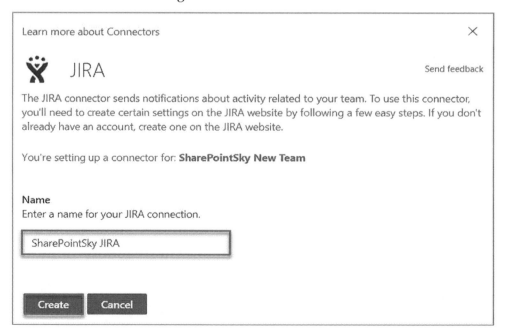

3. Once the new JIRA account creation is done, the **JIRA** web part will appear on the modern site page as shown in the following screenshot:

List (preview)

The **List (preview)** web part helps you to view only one of the lists from all the lists which are present in your existing SharePoint site. Follow the given steps to add this web part: Note: At the time of writing this book, it was still in preview, but now you may find like "List"

1. If you want to view your list in the modern SharePoint site page, add the **List (preview)** web part by using the search box:

2. When you click on the **List (preview)** web part, a **List** dialog box appears on the screen where you need to select a list that you want to add to this modern site page, as shown in the following screenshot:

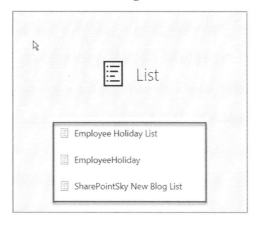

3. After selecting your specific list from the **List** dialog box, the list will be seen on the modern site page as shown below.

4. On the modern site page only, you can perform all the operations in the List such as adding a new item, editing the existing item, etc.

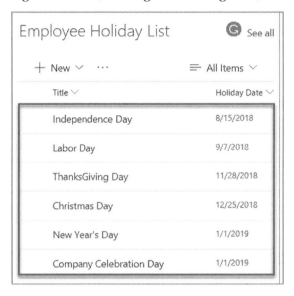

News

By using the **News** web part, you can show the latest news which you need to add to this web part. To add this web part, follow the given steps:

1. To add the **News** web part, click on the + option and then click on the **News** web part. You can easily find this web part by typing in the search box:

2. When you click on the **News** web part, the screen looks like as shown in the following screenshot. To add the latest news in the web part, make sure that the page is published so that you can add the news in the publishing mode.

3. To add the latest news, click on the **+Add** drop-down option and choose whether you want to add **News post** or **News link** as shown in the screenshot given below.

4. You can also give the News title at the top of the web part as shown in the following screenshot:

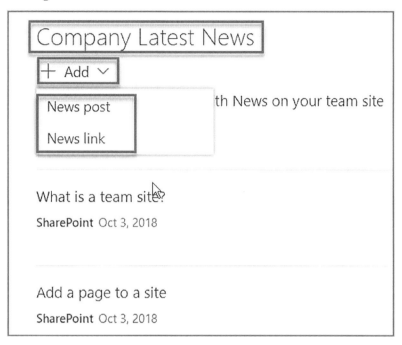

5. When you click on **News post**, a new site page appears on the screen. On this site page, you can type your latest news and you can also design the page by using the other web part. Then, click on **Post news**:

6. Once the news gets posted, the page will look like as shown in the following screenshot:

Properties

If you want to add more design to the **news** web part, there are some properties present in the news settings page. To add the properties, click on the **Edit** mode of the **news** web part. Then, you can see the edit page on the right-hand side of the existing page.

The two sites present are as follows:

*   **This site:** By using this option, the news will appear only on this site page.

*   **Select sites:** By using this option, the news will appear only for those sites which you choose as per your choice.

Similarly, there are four types of layouts which are as follows:

*   **Top story:** If you choose this layout, the **news** web part will look like as shown in the following screenshot:

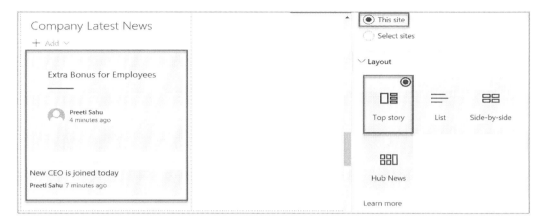

- **List:** If you choose the **List** layout, the **News** web part will appear like a list as shown in the following screenshot. In this layout, you can also choose the number of news items to be shown.

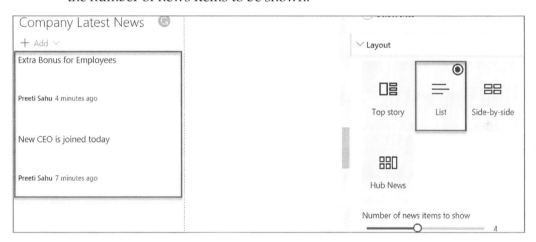

- **Side-by-side**: If you choose this layout, the news web part will look like as shown in the following screenshot:

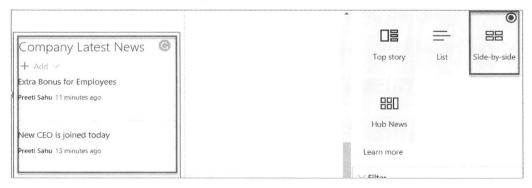

- **Hub News:** If you choose the **Hub News** layout, the news web part will look like a Hub type which is shown in the following screenshot:

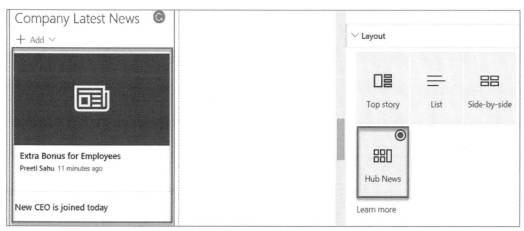

There is another property named **Filter**. If you want to filter out some latest news, you can use this filter property. By using this **Filter** option, you can easily get the filter news:

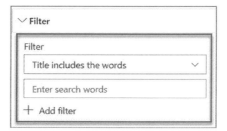

Microsoft Forms

Microsoft Form is nothing but a survey form which helps you to share ideas and collect feedback from your organization. By using this web part, you can get results, make voting fun or show a group of how everyone is performing as a whole on a topic quiz. To add this web part, follow the given steps:

1. To add the **Microsoft Forms** web part, click on the **+** option and then click on the **Microsoft Forms** web part. You can easily find this web part by typing in the search box:

2. Once you click on the web part, it will ask you to create surveys, quizzes and polls by using **New form**.

3. If you have already created this form before and if you want to create this form in the existing form, click on **Add existing form**:

4. When you click on **New form**, the **Microsoft Forms** dialog box appears on the existing page where you need to enter the new form name. Then, click on **Create**:

5. After clicking on the **Create** button, the form will look like as shown in the following screenshot. You can change the name of the form by clicking on the form name:

6. When you click on the form name, the form appears as shown in the following screenshot. You can also provide an image to the survey form by using the **Insert image** icon which is present on the right-hand side of the form name.

7. If you want to give the description of the new form, you can give the description by using the form description field:

8. To add a question to the Microsoft Forms web part, click on the **+Add question** button. When you click on the button, it will ask you to choose the voting icons as follows:

- Choice

- Text

- Rating

- Date

- … (Rating, Likert, Next Promoter Score)

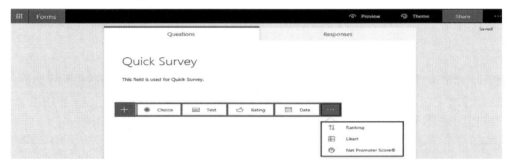

9. When you select one of the voting icons, it will ask you to add a question in the question field. As shown in the following screenshot, it was choosing the rating icon, so it is displaying star symbol. Here, you can change your symbol from the **Symbol** drop-down menu and also change levels from the **Levels** drop-down menu.

10. At the top of the page, the four important options displayed are as follows:

- **Copy:** If you want to copy the question, you can use this copy option.

- **Delete:** If you want to remove the question from Microsoft Forms, you can use this delete option.

- **Move up:** This option is used for ordering purpose. If you want to move the question up one position in the list of questions, you can change the order of the question by using the upward arrow symbol.

- **Move down:** In the same way, if you want to move the question down one position in the list of questions, you can change the order of the question by using the downward arrow symbol.

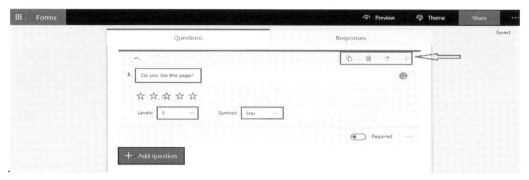

Properties

There are four properties of Microsoft Forms which are present at the top of the forms. The four properties are as follows:

- Preview

- Theme

- Share

- … (More)

Let's discuss these properties in detail.

Preview

Preview helps you to view the **Microsoft Forms** web part before it is acquired in your site page. When you submit this form, the owner will be able to see your name and email address. By clicking on the **Back** option, you can go to Microsoft Forms as shown in the following screenshot:

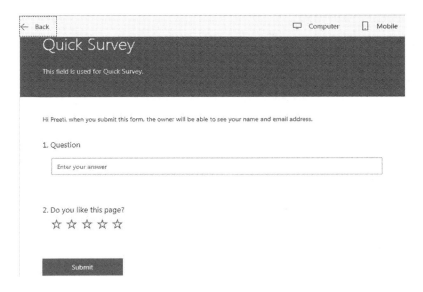

Theme

Theme helps you to provide a background theme to the **Microsoft Forms** web part which makes the form look better. When you click on the theme option, it asks you to choose a particular theme as shown below.

If you want to show more themes, click on the **+** option and then click on the **Theme** option:

Share

You can share the Microsoft Forms link within your organization by using various options as follows:

- Link
- Embed
- Message, Mail, etc.

If you want to send the Microsoft Forms link as a template, then click on **+Get a link to duplicate** and follow the steps.

If you want to send the Microsoft Forms link as collaborate, then click on **+Get a link to view and edit** and follow the steps.

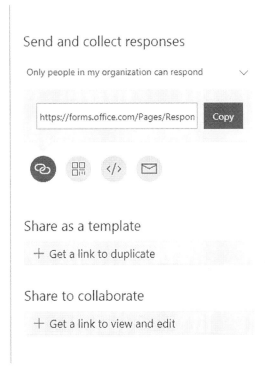

... (More)

When you click on the ... option which represents as more, it displays the options as shown in the following screenshot:

1. When you edit the Microsoft Forms in the modern site page, a form dialog box appears on the existing site page as shown in the following screenshot.

2. If you want to modify or edit the form, then click on **Edit current form**. It will directly go to the Microsoft Forms web part. **Form web address** will look like as shown in the following screenshot.

3. If you want to collect the responses of the survey form, then choose the **Collect responses** option and click on the **OK** button:

4. If you want to choose the **Show form results** option, by default the option will be selected as **A web address will be created. Anyone with it can view a summary of responses**. Then, click on **OK**:

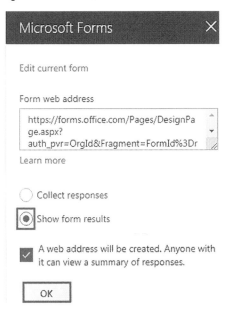

5. Once the form editing and the page publishing is done, you can see the survey form/Microsoft Forms as shown in the following screenshot:

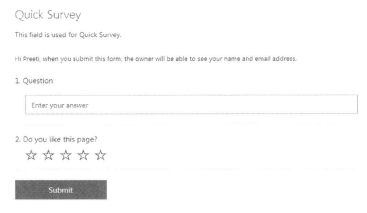

6. In the preceding screenshot, I chose the first survey symbol as a text; hence, you should give the response by using the text box only, and the second survey symbol as a star, so you should give the response by using the star rating.

Office 365 videos

The **Office 365 video** web part helps you to display an Office 365 video on your page. To add this web part, follow the given steps:

7. To add the **Office 365 video** web part, click on the + option and then click on **Office 365 video**. You can easily find this web part by typing in the search box:

8. When you click on the **Office 365 video** web part, it appears on the page as shown in the following screenshot. Click on the **Add video** option or go to the **Edit** mode of this web part:

9. When you click on **Add video**, an **Office 365 video** dialog box appears on the existing page. In this box, you will be asked to find the video you want to add to the Office 365 video portal and then paste its web address in the **Video address** box.

10. If you want to show the title of the video and video info, then enable the **Show title and video info** option as shown in the following screenshot:

11. After filling all these properties, you can view the Office 365 video with the title and video info in your modern site page. You can also type the video **Caption** in this web part as shown in the following screenshot:

People

The **People** web part allows you to display the profile information by adding their custom links and description of each person. To add the People web part, follow the given steps:

1. To add the **People** web part, click on the **+** option and then click on **People**:

2. After you add the **People** web part, a **People profiles** box appears on the screen as shown in the following screenshot:

3. Here, you can edit this web part. By clicking on the edit option mode, you can change the title. I have changed the **People profiles** title to **Company Team Members**. Then, give your username as the team member. Here, it will directly show you the username and then select it as shown in the following screenshot:

4. Here, details of one member is BijaySahoo. Similarly, you can enter more number of user details by using the **People** web part:

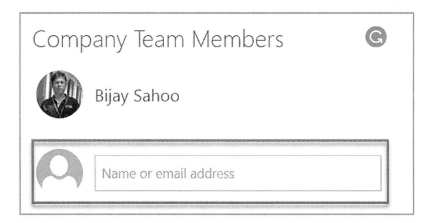

5. If you want to remove/delete the user profile, go to **People profiles** of the **People** web part. Then, click on the **X** (remove profile) icon which is present at the top-right corner of the user profile. When you click on the **X** icon, the user profile will be removed from the web part:

6. If you want to drag/move this user profile to a new location, then go to **People profiles** of the **People** web part. Then, click on the **Drag profile to a new location** icon which is present at the bottom-right corner of the user profile. When you click on **Drag profile to a new location**, the user will be dragged to a new location in the web part:

7. If you want to add some more designs to the People web part, follow the given steps:

    1. First, select the **People** web part and then click on the **Edit Web Part** option.

2. When you click on the **Edit** option, a **People** layout box appears on the right-hand side of the web part. Here, you can see that there are two layouts. First, select the **Compact** Layout as shown in the following screenshot.

3. If you select the **Compact** Layout, the **People** web part will be displayed vertically as shown in the following screenshot:

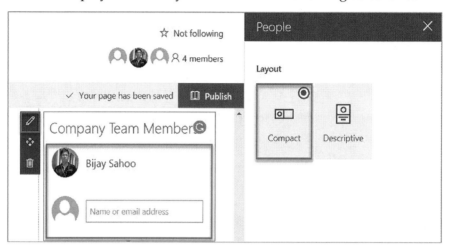

8. Now, select the **Descriptive** layout option. After selecting the **Descriptive** layout, the web part will look like as shown in the following screenshot where you can give some description about the user:

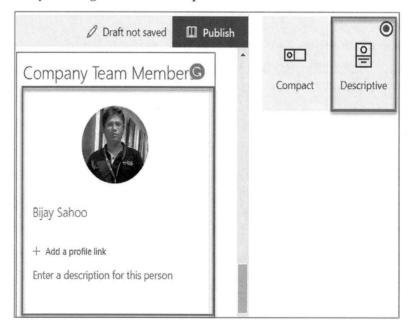

9. As shown in the following screenshot, you can even add a profile link. Just click on the **Add a Profile link** option and insert the address in the **Address** text box. Now, click on the **Save** button:

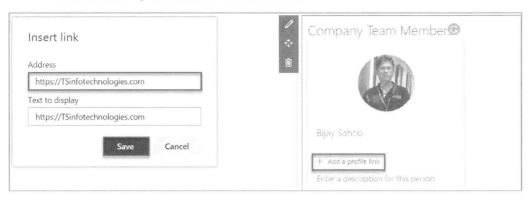

10. You can also add the description about the user. I have given the description about the user whose name is BijaySahoo:

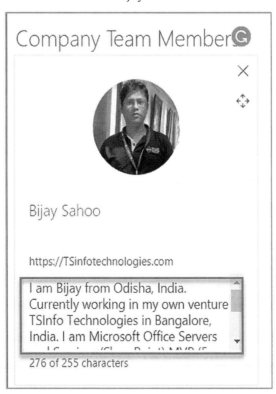

11. After publishing the modern site page, the **People** web part will be displayed as shown in the given screenshot:

Company Team Members

Bijay Sahoo

https://TSinfotechnologies.com

I am Bijay from Odisha, India. Currently working in my own venture TSInfo Technologies in Bangalore, India. I am Microsoft Office Servers and Services (Sh

Preeti Sahu

I am Preeti Sahu from Odisha, a developer of Microsoft SharePoint. Currently I am working with an organization (TSinfotechnologies pvt. ltd.) in Bangalore.

12. If you hover your mouse over the image of the user, you will see all the details of the user such as the email ID, phone number, LinkedIn profile, etc:

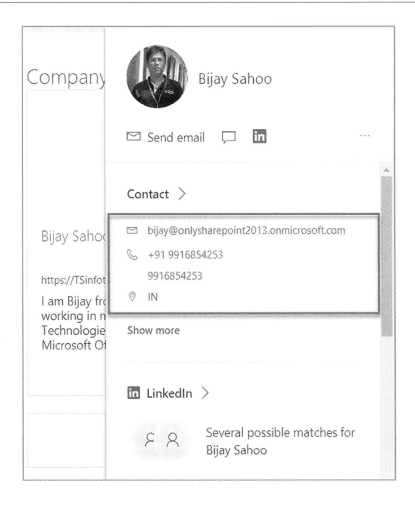

Power BI

The **Power BI** web part allows you to easily embed an interactive Power BI report on your page. To add this web part, follow the given steps:

1. To add the **Power BI** web part, click on the + option and then click on **Power BI**. You can easily find this web part by typing in the search box:

2. When you click on the **Power BI** web part, the web part looks like as shown in the following screenshot. To add the report, click on **Add report** and you will be asked to insert the Power BI report link:

Quick Chart

The **Quick Chart** web part helps you to create a pictorial representation of data through a bar or pie chart in the modern SharePoint site. To add this web part, follow the given steps:

1. To add the **Quick chart** web part, click on the + option and then click on the **Quick chart** web part. You can easily find this web part by typing in the search box:

2. After adding the **Quick chart** web part, the screen looks like as shown in the following screenshot. Then, go to the **Edit** mode of **Quick chart** web part. Here, a **Layout** option appears on the screen and here you need to select the **Quick chart**.

3. Here, you can see two layout options named **Column** and **Pie**. Select **Column** and the Quick chart web part appears as shown in the given screenshot:

4. After choosing the **Column** chart, enter all the data in the **Data label** field and the value in the **Value** field in the **Quick chart** settings. Here, I want two fields under **Data** in the **Data label** and **value** field also. So I can add Product and **Showcase** under the **Data label** by using the **+Add** option.

5. Similarly, you can add multiple data fields as shown in the following screenshot. In the following screenshot, you can see the diagrammatic representation of the data labels of **Product** and **Showcase**:

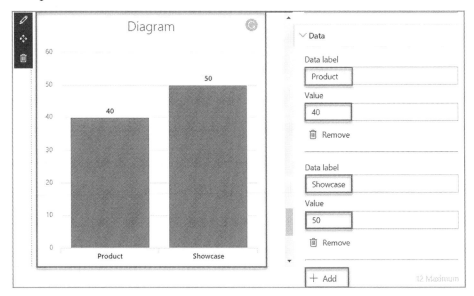

6. Similarly, if you choose the **Pie** layout, it will display the following pie chart. Here also you can enter the **Data Label** and **Value** as per your requirement by using the **+Add** option. Then, you will see the diagrammatic representation of the data in the form of a **Pie** chart as shown in the following screenshot:

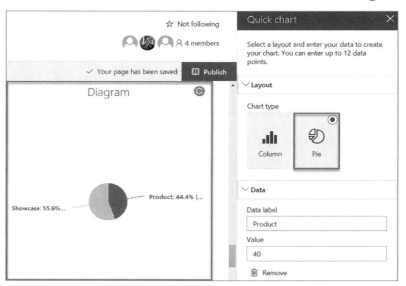

7. I chose the **Layout** option as **Column**, so here the **Data** value shows the data column wise as I have entered D**ata label** as **Product** and **Value** as 40. Similarly, in the second instance, I chose **Data label** as Showcase and **Value** as 50 as shown in the following screenshot:

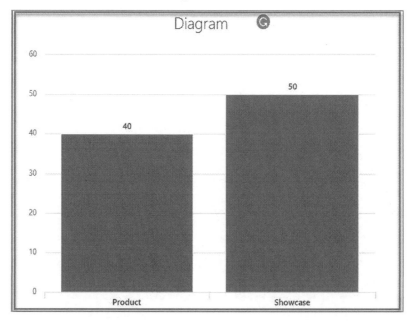

Quick Links

To add the **Quick links** web part, follow the given steps:

1. Click on the **+** option and then click on the **Quick links** web part. This web part helps you to add the links to important documents and pages. You can easily find this web part by typing in the search box:

2. After adding the **Quick links** web part, the screen looks like as shown below. Now, go to the **Edit** mode of the **Quick links** web part. Here, the **Layout** option appears under the **Quick links** layout.

There are six layouts having different properties as follows:

-   **Compact:** If you select the **Compact** layout, then in the site page, the **Quick links** property will appear as shown in the following screenshot:

-   **Filmstrip:** Here, if you select the **Filmstrip** layout, the view will display links with a slider in that site page:

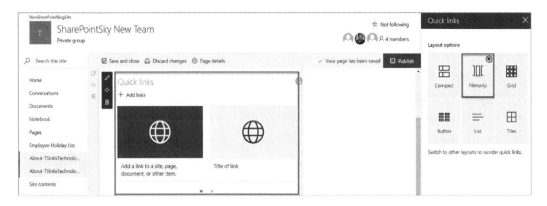

- **Grid:** If you select the **Grid** layout, the quick links will appear like a grid as shown in the given screenshot:

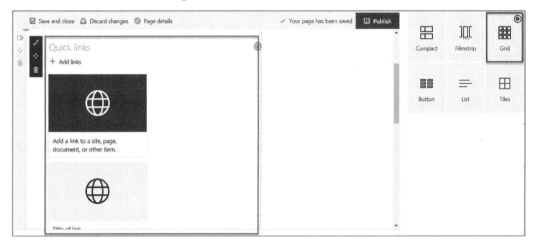

- **Button:** When you click on the **Button** layout, the quick links appear like the button view. Here, you can see the other options such as:

- **Show Description:** If you want to show the description in button quick links, then enable this option or else disable this option.

- **Icons**: You can change the icon button as per your choice like on left, on right etc.

- **Button appearance**: If you want the button appearance as Outline or Inline, then select this from the drop-down menu as per your choice.

- **Alignment**: Choose the alignment if you want to keep it to the top or center.

- **Title text**: Choose a title text if you want to keep it on one line or on two lines as per your choice.

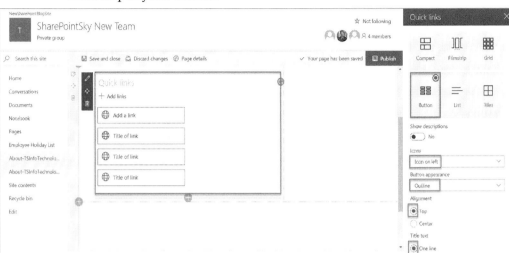

- **List:** When you click on the **List** layout, the Quick links web part appears like a list as shown in the following screenshot. Here, you can see the other options as follows:

- **Show description**: If you want to show the description in the list quick links, enable this option or else disable it.

- **Show icons**: If you want to show the icon in the Quick links, then enable this option or else disable it.

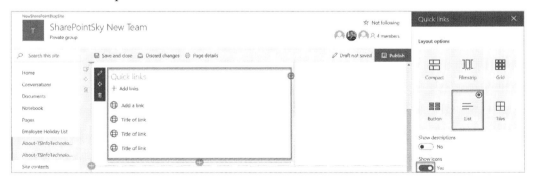

- **Tiles:** When you click on the **Tiles** layout, it appears as the tiles view as shown in the following screenshot. If you want to give a proper size, go to the **Icon size** properties and specify your size according to your choice.

If you want to show only the icon or image, then enable the Show only icon or image option as or disable it.

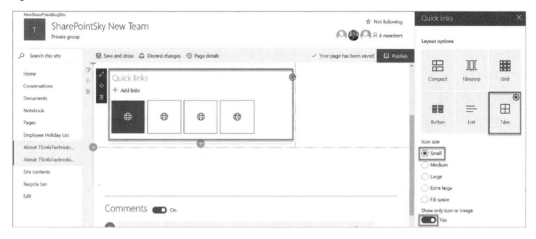

1. I chose the **Filmstrip** option, so it displays as shown below. Here, you can give the title instead of **Quick links.** I have given the title as **Quick Polls**. Then, click on the **+Add links** to add the new links.

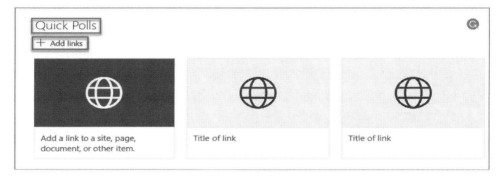

2. When you click on the **+Add links** option, a change item page appears where you need to change the image. Here, you can upload the image you want by using the **Recent, OneDrive, Site, Upload,** and **From a link**.

3. I have uploaded an image by using the **Upload** option and then clicked on the **Add item** button to add the image as shown in the following screenshot:

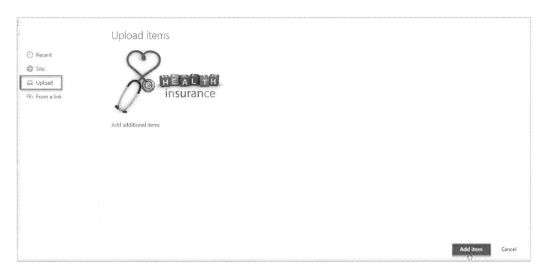

4. Then, after the image is uploaded in the **Quick links** web part, go to the **Edit** mode of the uploaded image. Here, the **Quick links** settings page will appear on the right-hand side of the existing site page.

5. In the settings page, you can see the link. If you want to change the link, click on the **Change** option. Similarly, you can give the **Title**. I have given the title **Health insurance**.

6. You can choose the **Thumbnail** option if you want **Auto-selected**, **Custom image**, or **Icon** as per your choice.

7. You can give an alternative text field for the thumbnail image:

8. By following the above steps, you can add one or more number of images. Further, if you want to add another image, then click on the **+ Add links** option and follow the above step s:

9. Once the site page publishing is done, you can see **Quick links** and their titles in the slide show as shown in the following screenshot:

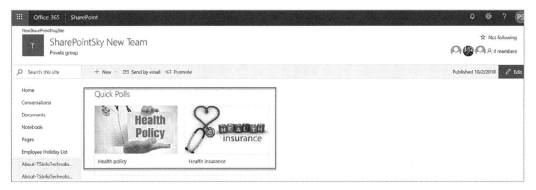

Site activity

The **Site activity** web part helps you to show all the activities on your existing site such as create, modify, share, etc. To add this web part, follow the given steps:

1. To add the **Site activity** web part, click on the **+** option and then click on **Site activity**. You can easily find this web part by typing in the search box:

2. When you click on the **Site activity** web part, it appears on the modern site page as shown in the given screenshot. In this screenshot, you can view some of the site activities which you did before.

3. If you want to see all the site activities at a time, click on the **See all** option which is present in the web part:

4. When you click on the **See all** option, it displays all the site activities on the page as shown in the following screenshot:

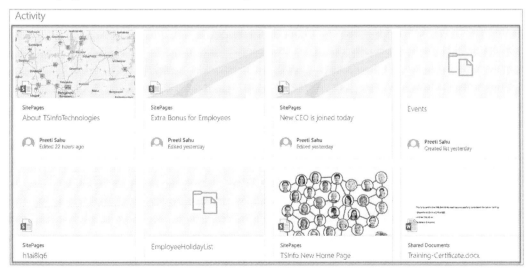

Properties

There is one property present in the **Site activity** web part. To see the property, go to the **Edit** mode of that web part. When you click on the **Edit** option, a site activity setting page appears in that existing page, where you need to specify a number to show the items at a time as shown below:

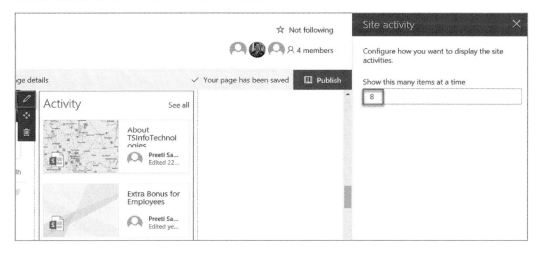

Sites

By using the **Sites** web part, you can view all the SharePoint sites as per your choice in your modern site age. To add the web part, follow the given steps:

1. To add the **Sites** web part, click on the + option and then click on the **Sites** option. You can easily find this web part by typing in the search box:

2. When you click on the **Sites** web part, it appears like a site frame where you need to add SharePoint sites as per your needs. So, to add the sites, click on the **+Add** option, and you can go to the **Edit** mode of the Sites web part as shown below. You can also give the site title in the **Sites** web part:

3. When you click on the **+Add** option, the Sites settings page appears on the screen. Here, you need to select your sites based on the requirements. To get the sites faster, you can search the sites from the search box. Then, the selected sites will be available in the modern site page:

Properties

If you want to provide some extra design to the **Sites** web part, go to the **Edit** mode of that web part. In the edit mode, there are two layouts which are as follows:

- **Filmstrip:** When you select the **Filmstrip** layout, the **Sites** web part will be displayed like a strip as shown in the following screenshot:

- **Cards:** When you select the **Cards** layout, the **Sites** web part will be displayed as shown in the following screenshot:

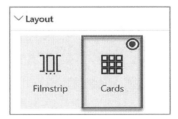

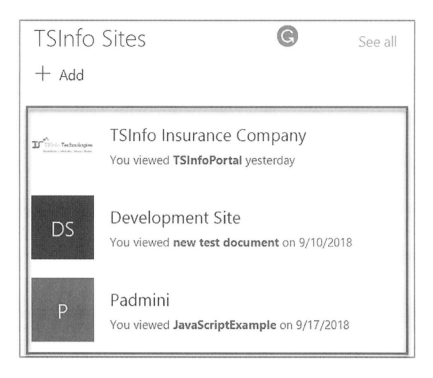

Twitter (preview)

The Twitter web part helps you to show tweets which are relevant to you or your audience right on your page.

Note: During the time of writing this book, Twitter web part is in Preview and very soon, it will be updated by Microsoft

To add this web part, follow the given steps:

1. To add the **Twitter (preview)** web part, click on the **+** option and then click on the **Twitter** or you can easily find this web part by typing in the search box:

2. When you click on the **Twitter (preview)** web part, it displays the Microsoft tweets as shown in following screenshot. Here also you can give the title of the twitter. If you want to know about the properties, then go to the **Edit** mode of that web part:

Properties

In the following screenshot, you can see a dialog box where you need to add the options as follows:

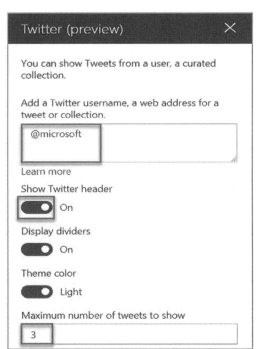

The following options are present in the dialog box:

- **Add a Twitter username, a web address for a tweet or collection:** This option helps you to add a web address or username for a tweet or collection.

- **Show Twitter header:** If you want to show the Twitter header, then enable this option or else disable it.

- **Display dividers:** If you want to display the Twitter dividers, then enable this option or else disable it.

- **Theme color:** If you want to display the Twitter theme color as light, then enable this option or else disable it.

- **Maximum number of tweets to show:** In this option, specify the number of tweets you want to show.

Now, the Twitter web part will be displayed vertically as shown in the following screenshot:

Like **the Tweet:** If you want to like the Twitter page, then click on the **Like** symbol as shown in the following screenshot:

Share the Tweet: If you want to share the Twitter page, then click on the share symbol as shown below:

Weather

The **Weather** web part in the modern site page provides the weather information of a particular area. To add this web part, follow the given steps:

1. To add the **Weather** web part, click on the + option and then click on **Weather** or you can easily find this web part by typing in the search box:

2. When you click on the **Weather** web part, you will be asked to enter the location for which you want to know the weather information. When you enter the location with the help of the search box, it will directly show you the weather information of that particular place as shown in the following screenshot:

Properties

To know the property of the **Weather** web part, go to the **Edit** mode of that web part and click on the **Display temperature as** property. In this property, there are two options:

- **Fahrenheit:** If you select this option, the weather temperature will be displayed in Fahrenheit.

- **Celsius:** If you select this option, the weather temperature will be displayed in Celsius.

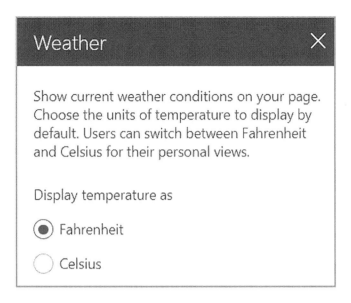

Yammer

The **Yammer** is an **Enterprise Social Network (ESN)** which helps you to communicate with the inside user or outside user of your organization.

Microsoft provides **Yammer** web part to display **Yammer** feeds in SharePoint Online modern site.

To add this web part, follow the given steps:

1. To add the **Yammer** web part, click on the + option and then click on **Yammer** or you can easily find this web part by typing in the search box:

2. When you click on the **Yammer** web part, you will be asked to add a group for your conversation. So, to add a group in the Yammer web part, click on the **Add a group** button:

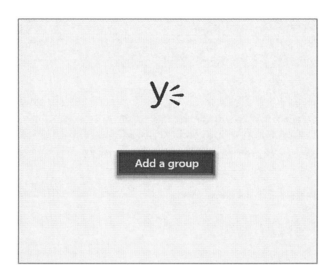

3. When you click on the Add a group button, a Yammer settings page appears in the existing page.

4. Enter groups in the Type to search a Yammer group box and then choose the conversations to show **Top conversations, Latest conversations** or **Only conversations you choose** as shown in the following screenshot:

5. Now, you can see the **Yammer** group and its conversations in the modern site page as shown in the following screenshot. You can also give the Yammer **Title** at the top of the web part:

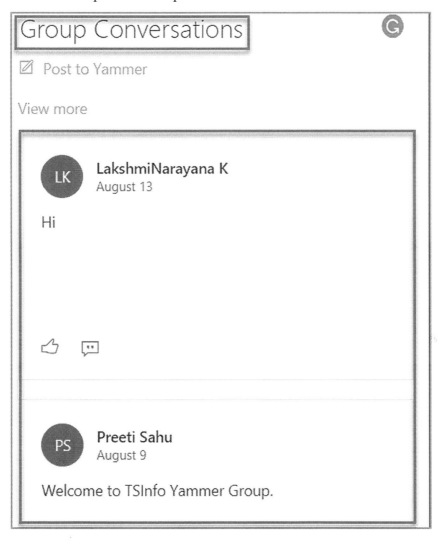

Timer

The Timer web part is the latest feature of the modern SharePoint page. This web part helps you to display the time (Count up and Countdown) of an event:

1. Search the **Countdown Timer** from the search box and click on it to add it to the modern page.

2. When you add this Timer web part, it displays as shown in the following screenshot. Here, you can add **Title** and **Description** of the timer.

3. Then, click on the **Edit** option to edit this timer.

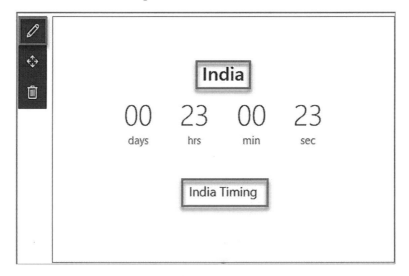

4. When you click on the **Edit** option, a dialogue box appears where you need to fill the following fields:

    *   **Count down:** If you want the time as count down, then select this option.

    *   **Count up:** If you want to the time as count up, then select this option.

    *   **Display timer as:** Select the type of the timer you want to display such as (Days), (Days, hours, minutes) or (Days, hours, minutes, seconds).

    *   **Call to action:** If you want to insert any action, then enable this option as **On**.

- **Call to action text:** Enter some text to call the action.

- **Call to action link:** Enter the URL address to call the action.

- **Background image:** If you want to add the background image of the timer, then click on **Add** and **Upload** the image. You can also **Change** and **Remove** the background image.

- **Overlay color:** To overlay the color, select any option from the drop-down menu.

- **Overlay opacity:** A semi transparent color overlay is added to help with text legibility.

5. Once you publish the modern SharePoint site page, you can view the count-down timer web part as shown in the following screenshot.

Markdown

The Markdown web part is a purely new web part which helps you to add text to your modern page and format it by using the Markdown language. To add this web part, find the web part by typing **Markdown** in the search box and then click on it:

After adding this web part to the page, the **Markdown** web part will be displayed as a black box. You need to insert your text content inside the box. You can take a look at the following screenshot to see how this web part looks like:

This **Markdown** web part has some properties which you can see in the following screenshot:

The properties are as follows:

- **B (Bold):** This symbol helps to make your text bold.
- **I (Italic):** This symbol helps to make your text italic.
- **Strikethrough:** This symbol is known as strikethrough.

Once you click on this symbol, it will look as shown in the following screenshot:

To know the company details, Click below link: https://www.tsinfotechnologies.com/~~~~

- **Insert Link:** This symbol helps you to insert a link to the text.

When you click on the symbol, an insert link box appears as shown below. It has some fields as follows:

- **Address:** Enter the URL address of the text.
- **Text to display**: When you enter the URL address in the **Address** link, this field will automatically appear with the same name as Address.
- **Open link in a new tab:** To view this link in another tab, check this field.

Once you fill all the fields, click on **Save**.

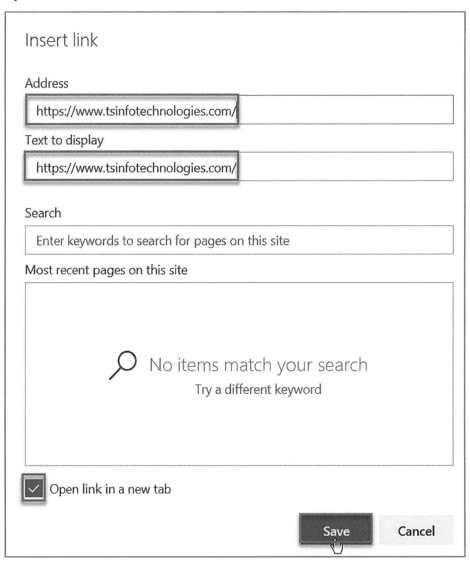

- **Theme:** This option helps you to change the theme or background of your text. It has two options:

- **Light theme:** Click on the **Light theme** as shown below.

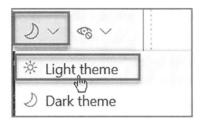

When you click on this option, the text will be displayed in the light theme as shown below:

```
To know the company details, Click below
link:
[https://www.tsinfotechnologies.com
/](https://www.tsinfotechnologies.com/)
```

- **Dark theme:** Click on the **Dark theme** as shown below:

When you click on this option, the text will be displayed in the dark theme as shown below:

```
To know the company details, Click below
link:
[https://www.tsinfotechnologies.com
/](https://www.tsinfotechnologies.com/)
```

- **Preview:** This option helps you to display the text as preview or hide the preview. This option has two types of preview:

- **Show preview:** This preview helps you to display the text with preview. Click on the **Show preview** option.

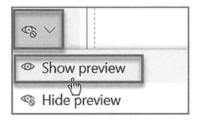

When you click on this option, the screen looks like as shown in the following screenshot:

- **Hide preview:** This preview helps you to hide the text that you inserted. Click on the **Hide preview** option.

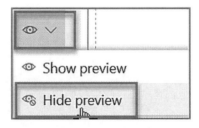

Once you click on this option, the screen will be displayed as shown in the following screenshot:

```
To know the company details, Click below
link:
[https://www.tsinfotechnologies.com
/](https://www.tsinfotechnologies.com/)
```

Now, publish the modern site page. Once the publishing is done, the Markdown option will appear on the screen as shown in the following screenshot:

To know the company details, Click below link:
https://www.tsinfotechnologies.com/

Summary

In this chapter, we learned about the various web parts that you can use inside a page in SharePoint Online modern sites. In the next chapter, we will take a look at the various SharePoint Online modern portals that we created by adding various web parts.

CHAPTER 8

SharePoint Online Modern Site Design Examples

The modern site design prefers to design a site page as per your own custom configurations. In this chapter, you will learn how to design a page by using various types of modern web parts. You can take a look at different site design portals which I have designed by using different types of modern web parts in SharePoint Online.

Let us see a few SharePoint Online modern site design examples.

Portal 1 – TSInfo New — a software development portal company portal

The following modern UI portal consists of 13 web parts. To know more about this portal, let us take a look at the following points:

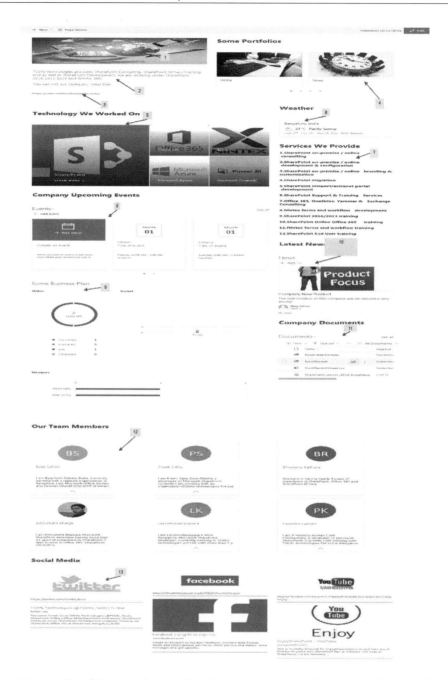

- **Image**: In this portal, number 1 represents the image web part. This web part helps to add an image from the different options such as recent, web search, OneDrive, sites and so on. You can also add a caption under the image.

- **Text**: Number 2 represents the text web part where you can type some text, paragraph, etc. You can also make a design by using some additional properties of the text web part which is already mentioned above.

- **Link**: Number 3 represents the link web part which helps to display any image, video or any text by using only the hyperlink URL. By clicking on this link, the end user can visit the URL site.

- **Quick links**: Number 4 represents the quick links web part which helps to add the links to the important documents and pages. By clicking only once on the link, the end user can visit that specific website.

- **Hero**: Number 5 represents the hero web part. By using this hero web part, you can display up to five items with compelling images, texts and links to draw attention to each item. If you want to show five items at a time with some text, images and links, then you can easily use this web part.

- **Weather**: Number 6 represents the weather web part which helps to provide the weather information of a specific place. If you want to know about the current weather information, then you can use this web part.

- **Text**: As discussed in Number 2, the text web part helps to add some text or paragraph. So, you can use this web part to add text or paragraph only.

- **Events**: The Events web part helps to show all the events of your organization, so that people can get to know when a particular event is going on. So, Number 8 represents the event web part. By using this web part, you can add a number of upcoming events of your organization.

- **Quick chart**: Number 9 represents the quick chart web part which helps to create a pictorial representation of data through a bar or pie chart in the modern SharePoint site. By using this web part, you can display your data/ records of a specific task.

- **News**: Number 10 represents the news web part which helps to add some latest news of an organization. By using this web part, you can update with yourself.

- **Document library (preview)**: Number 11 represents a document library (preview) web part. By using this web part, you can easily upload and modify your documents in the existing site page only.

- **People**: Number 12 represents the people web part. The people web part displays the profile information of a group of selected people by adding their custom links and description of each person.

- **Link**: As discussed in number 3, the link web part is used to display any image, video or any text by using only the hyperlink URL. So, number 13 represents the link web part. In this portal, by using this link web part, it displays **Twitter**, **Facebook** and **YouTube**.

Portal 2 – TSInfo New Home Page

This is another portal where you can see the following types of web parts:

- Image as it is present in the header part of the portal

- Embed web part as **Business Team Meeting**

- Events web part as **Upcoming Team Events**

- Quick chart web part as a graphical bar representation of **Blog Details**

- Document library web part in the slide show view as **Company Documents**

- Image gallery web part as **Quick links**

- Sites web part which shows all the current sites of **SharePoint Sites**

- Person web part as **Our Team**

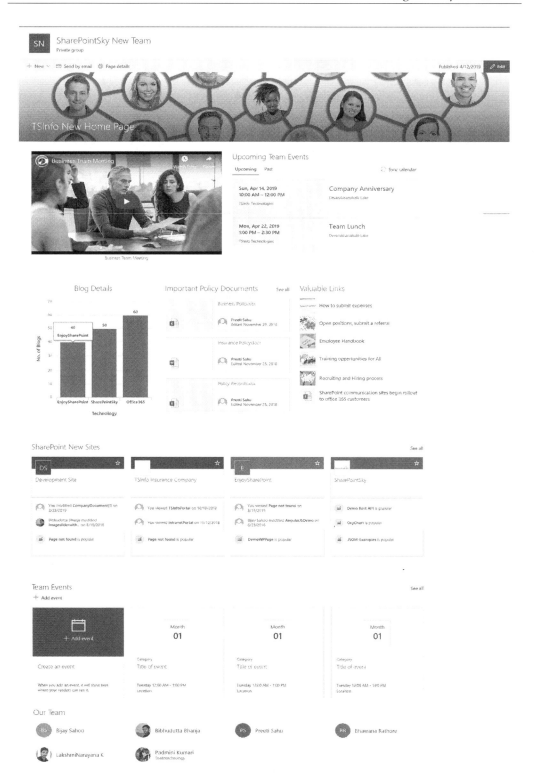

Portal 3 – TSInfo Technologies

In this portal, you can see other various types of web parts as follows:

- Image as it is present in the header part of the portal

- Event web part as **Upcoming Events**

- News web part as **Announcements**

- Link as **Learn Microsoft SharePoint 2016**

- Image gallery as **Clever Tools** with the slide show view

- Person as the **Employees of the month**

- Bing maps web part represents the current location which shows **Our Headquarters**

- Link web part which represents SharePoint related stuff

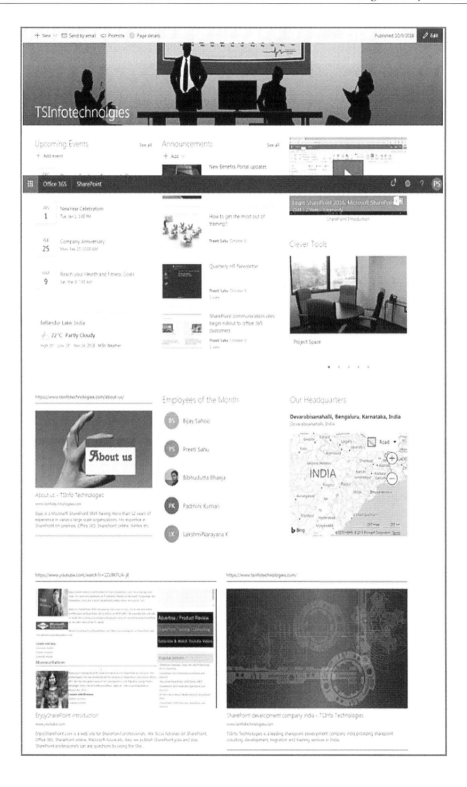

Portal 4 – About TSInfoTechnologies

The fourth portal represents some extra web parts as follows:

- Image as it is present in the header part of the portal
- Recent documents web part represents all the current documents as **Most Recent Documents**
- Bing maps web part as **Company Venue**
- Document library web part as **SharePointSky New Documents**
- Image gallery web part as **Gallery**
- List web part as **Employee Holiday List**
- **GitHub** web part
- **JIRA** web part
- **Twitter** web part
- Site activity web part as **Activity**
- Yammer web part as **Group Conversations**
- Site web part as **TSInfo Sites**

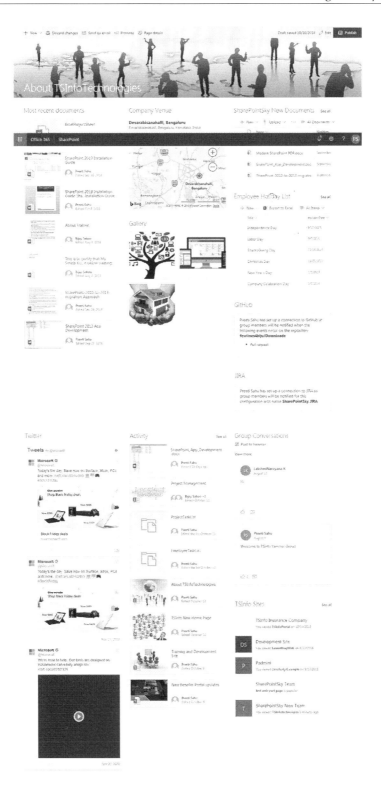

Portal 5 – Training and Development Site

The fifth portal represents the following web parts:

- Image as it is present in the header part of the portal
- Hero web part which directly displays five items at a time
- News web part as **Recent Updates**
- Event web part as **Latest Events**
- Yammer web part as **Team Conversations**
- Sites as **Recent Sites**

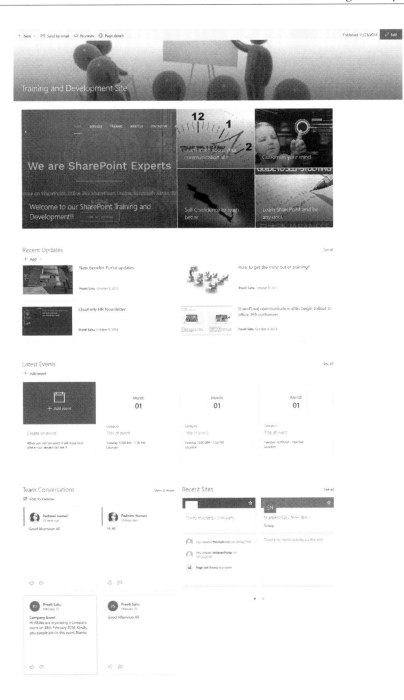

Portal 6 – the Project Management page

The *sixth* portal represents the **Project Management** page, where you can see that the web parts are related to the project as follows:

- Image as it is present in the header part of the portal

- List web part as **ProjectList, ProjectTaskList, Pending Task, Completed Task**

- An image web part with some caption

- Quick chart web part as **Project Chart** which displays a pie chart

- Person as **Project Team Members**

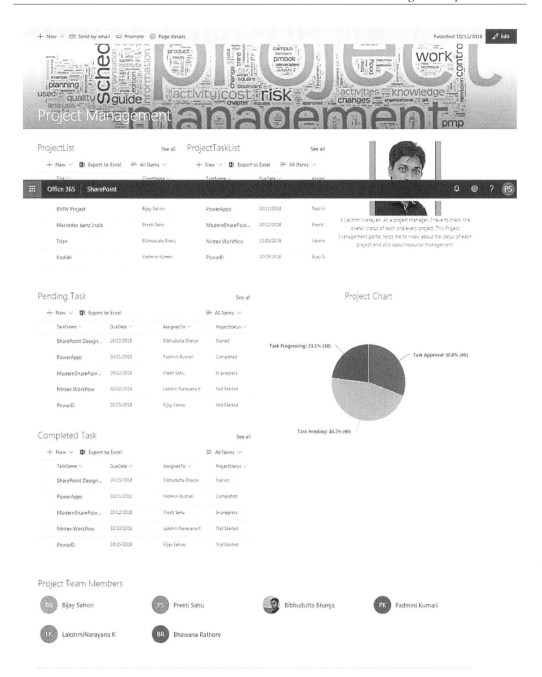

Portal 7 – the New Insurance page

The seventh portal represents the **New Insurance** page where you can see that the web parts are related to insurance as follows:

- Image as it is present in the header part of the portal

- **Quick Links**

- Image gallery web part as **Hot Updates**

- Image web part as **Tip of the Day, Home Insurance, Health Insurance, Cyber Secure Insurance** existing with some caption

- Microsoft videos as **Daily Updates**

- Microsoft forms as **Quick Polls**

- Text web part as **Suggestion Box**

+ New ∨   Send by email   Page details   Published 6/15/2018   ✎ Edit

New Insurance Page

Quick Links

Protection

Help

Security

Safety

Notification

Declaration   See all

+ New ∨ ···   ≡ All Items ∨

Title ∨   Deliver Da

Product Showcase   7/29/201

Product   7/26/201

Hot Updates

Updates

The Health Insurance Special

Health Insurance Policy

· · · ·

Announcements

1.The Showcase of the product is going
to deliver very soon.

2. The Company will share the Sample
product with a limited period of time.

Tip Of The Day

What's New?

1.The new SharePoint Online, available
with Office 365, includes a wide variety
of improvements and new features.
Discover how SharePoint Online can help
you share your work and work with
others, organize your projects and teams
and discover people and information.

2.New ways to work with video and rich
media (SharePoint Online in Office 365
Enterprise plans only)

Home Insurance

Home which is belonging from various events at very low
premium rate.

Health Insurance

Complete Health protection involved you and your family
against Hospital expenses.

Cyber Secure Insurance

Protection against multiple cyber risks like identity
theft,malware etc

Daily Updates

Suggestion Box

If you have a great idea for TS Insurance Company, We would like to
hear it so please contact with us by our Company Email ID or Contact
Number which is mentioned below-

Email ID- info@tsinfotechnologies.com

Contact No- +91 9916854253

Quick Polls

A ▦ QUICK POLL

Poll

Hi, when you submit this form, the owner will be able to see your name and email address.

* Required

1. How do you like this Insurance Page so far? *

Nice

Ok

Needs to Changes

Submit

This content is created by the owner of the form. The data you submit will be sent to the form
owner. Never give out your password.
Powered by Microsoft Forms | Privacy and Cookies

Portal 8 – the New TS Corporate portal

The eighth portal represents the **New TS Corporate Portal** page where you can see that the web parts are related to the corporate portal as follows:

- Image as it is present in the header part of the portal

- Image gallery web part as **Portrait**

- Quick chart web part as **Blueprint** which displays a graphical bar

- Bing maps web part as **Venue**

- Yammer web part for conversations

- Microsoft Forms web part as **Voting**

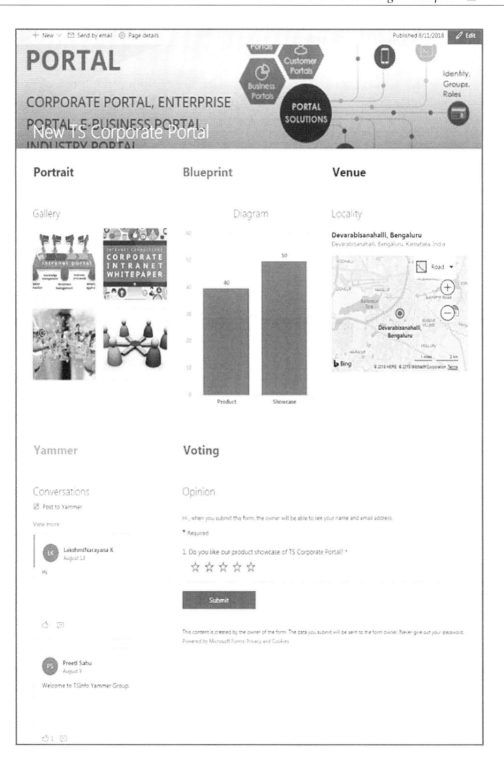

Summary

In this chapter, we learned about various modern team site portals and modules associated with them. This clearly depicts that using SharePoint Online; we can not only create a variety of online portals but also precisely manage content. In the next chapter, we will take a look at some new features of SharePoint 2019.

CHAPTER 9

SharePoint 2019 Modern Experience

In this chapter, we will learn about SharePoint Server 2019, various new features of SharePoint Server 2019, how to create a new modern team site in SharePoint Server 2019, and the difference in features between SharePoint Online modern team sites and modern SharePoint server 2019 team sites.

Microsoft released SharePoint 2019, the latest SharePoint On-Premises version. A lot of organizations are not willing to move to SharePoint Online. There can be many reasons such as they have some customizations which are not supported on SharePoint Online, or they are using some third-party solutions in SharePoint On-Premises which are not supported in SharePoint On-Premises, or they may have some compliance restrictions.

So, Microsoft is encouraging organizations to use the hybrid model. In a hybrid environment, organizations can move content which they want to SharePoint Online and they can store the remaining content in the on-premise environment.

According to Microsoft, in SharePoint Server 2019, Microsoft focused on team collaboration and user experiences across devices (like SharePoint Online Office 365).

SharePoint Server 2019 will deliver enhancements and new capabilities in the following three major areas:

- Modern, familiar and intuitive user experiences based on our investments in SharePoint Online
- New ways to engage with content across browsers and devices

- Robust scale, security and compliance capabilities to meet growing demands

Microsoft introduced modern SharePoint experience in SharePoint 2019, which has already released in Office 365 SharePoint Online:

- Now, in SharePoint 2019, a user can create modern team sites, communication sites, modern site pages, modern lists and modern document libraries which were there in SharePoint Online. Modern lists and document libraries have a very impressive UI and a lot of useful new enhanced features and they are responsive. The look and feel of the modern SharePoint experience is very good. So, if any organization is using a hybrid SharePoint environment, they will get a similar experience like SharePoint Online Office 365.

- SharePoint has been used in mobile devices in various organizations. SharePoint Server 2019 makes very easier, more intelligent, more personalized for mobile users.

- Now, SharePoint 2019 allows you to upload larger files compared to SharePoint 2016. In SharePoint 2019, users can upload files up to 15 GB in size. This is one step ahead for working with large files in SharePoint.

- In earlier versions of SharePoint, the URL path length was 260 characters, but now it has increased to 400 characters.

- Microsoft has removed a few character restrictions for file names and in SharePoint 2019 it allows # and % in files and folder names inside document libraries.

A few new features in SharePoint Server 2019

As SharePoint Server 2019 is built on the same platform of SharePoint online, you will see a lot of similar features of SharePoint Online. A few new and updated features are as follows:

- **Modern user experiences**: Like SharePoint Online, in SharePoint Server 2019, you can see the modern user experience. You will have a similar look and feel like SharePoint Online. Modern user experiences are easy to use and ensure reliability, performance, and security under real-world pressures of scale and complexity.

- **Modern team sites**: The same modern team site concept has been introduced in SharePoint server 2019. A modern team site connects you and the team across the organization. SharePoint server 2019 users will get a similar kind of user experience like the SharePoint Online team site.

- **Modern site pages**: Like SharePoint Online Office 365, SharePoint Server 2019 team site now has the modern site page. Modern pages is a great way to share ideas using images, Excel, Word and PowerPoint documents, embed video content, and more. You can create and publish attractive modern site pages quickly and easily, and they look great on any device. Modern pages are built with web parts, which you can customize according to your needs. You can add documents, embed videos, images, site activities, Yammer feeds, and more.

- **Modern list in SharePoint Server 2019**: SharePoint Online modern lists are already very popular among users for very attractive and useful features. Microsoft also introduced modern lists in SharePoint Server 2019. By using modern lists, teams can access, share, and collaborate with structured data and bring information from other systems to SharePoint to support a business process. People can create, curate, and interact with information with a rich set of capabilities that work across devices and browsers.

- **Modern libraries in SharePoint Server 2019**: SharePoint Server 2019 provides a better user experience for document libraries that is faster, more intuitive and responsive with modern document libraries. Modern document libraries have an updated user interface that offers an experience similar to OneDrive, so it's more intuitive to create a new folder and upload files in the browser.

- **Communication sites**: If you want to share a page with in your organization, the SharePoint communication site is a very good template to create the site. SharePoint Server 2019 also introduced the same communication sites which will allow you to communicate with people throughout your organization. Using communication sites, you can build beautiful, dynamic, mobile-ready communication sites and pages that will keep everyone informed and engaged.

Web Application in SharePoint 2019

A SharePoint web application is a collection of one or more websites configured to map the HTTP requests with a unique domain name. Each web application contains one or more site collections. Each web application creates a content database and authentication method to connect to a database. The default website is automatically created by IIS listens for incoming HTTP requests on port 80.

You can create additional IIS websites to provide additional HTTP entry points using different port numbers, different IP addresses, or different host headers.

When you create a web application in SharePoint, it creates an **IIS (Internet Information Services)** website with a root folder containing a web configuration file at location:C:\inetpub\wwwroot\wss\VirtualDirectories. You can also find the pool process for a web application once it is created from the IIS manager.

Create a web application in SharePoint 2019

To create a new site collection in SharePoint 2019, you need to first create a web application. Here, I will show you how to create a web application from the following:

- SharePoint 2019 central administration

- Using Microsoft PowerShell

Creating an application using SharePoint 2019 central administration

1. To create a web application, open SharePoint 2019 central administration and go to **Application Management** | **Manage Web Applications**.

2. Then, provide a name, enter the port number in the **Port** field, and click on the **Enable Windows Authentication** checkbox as shown in the following screenshot:

Create New Web Application

Warning: This page is not encrypted for secure communication. User names, passwords, and any other information will be sent in clear text. For more information, contact your administrator.

OK   Cancel

IIS Web Site
Choose between using an existing IIS web site or create a new one to serve the Microsoft SharePoint Foundations application.

If you select an existing IIS web site, that web site must already exist on all servers in the farm and have the same name, or this action will not succeed.

If you wish to create a new IIS web site, it will be automatically created on all servers in the farm. If the IIS settings that you wish to change to not shown here, you can use this option to create the basic site, then update it using the standard IIS tools.

☐ Use an existing IIS web site
   Default Web Site

☑ Create a new IIS web site
   Name
   SharePoint - 2723

   Port
   2723

   Host Header

   Path
   C:\inetpub\wwwroot\wss\VirtualDirecto

Security Configuration
If you choose to use Secure Sockets Layer (SSL), you must add the certificate on each server using the IIS administration tools. Until this is done, the web application will be inaccessible from this web site.

Allow Anonymous
☐ Yes
☑ No

Use Secure Sockets Layer (SSL)
☐ Yes
☑ No

Claims Authentication Types
Choose the type of authentication you want to use for this zone.

Negotiate (Kerberos) is the recommended security configuration to use with Windows authentication. If this option is selected, and Kerberos is not configured, NTLM will be used. For Kerberos, the application pool account needs to be Network Service or an account that has been configured by the domain administrator. NTLM authentication will work with any application pool account and with the default domain configuration.

Basic authentication method passes users' credentials over a network in an unencrypted form. If you select this option, ensure Secure Sockets Layer (SSL) is enabled.

ASP.NET membership and role providers are used to enable Forms Based Authentication (FBA) for this Web application. After you create an IIS Web application, additional configuration is required.

Trusted Identity Provider
Authentication enables federated users in this Web application. This authentication uses claims based model and the user is redirected to a login form for authentication.

Learn about configuring authentication.

☑ Enable Windows Authentication
   ☑ Integrated Windows authentication
      NTLM
   ☐ Basic authentication (credentials are sent in clear text)

☐ Enable Forms Based Authentication (FBA)
   ASP.NET Membership provider name

   ASP.NET Role manager name

☐ Trusted Identity provider
   There are no trusted identity providers defined.

Sign In Page URL
When Claims Based Authentication Types are enabled, a URL for redirecting the user to this Sign In page is required.

Learn about Sign In page redirection URL.

☑ Default Sign In Page
☐ Custom Sign In Page

Public URL
The public URL is the domain name for all sites that users will access in this SharePoint Web application. This URL address will be used in all links shown on pages within the web application. By default, it is set to the current server name and port.

https://go.microsoft.com/fwlink/?LinkId=114854

URL
http://TSINFOTECH:2723/

Zone
Default

Application Pool
Choose the application pool to use for the new web application. This defines the account and credentials that will be used by this service.

You can choose an existing application pool or create a new one.

☐ Use existing application pool

☑ Create new application pool
   Application pool name
   SharePoint - 2723
   Select a security account for this application pool
   TSINFOTech\admin ▼
   Register new managed account

Database Name and Authentication
Use of the default database server and database name is recommended for most cases. Refer to the administrator's guide for advanced scenarios where specifying database information is required.

Use of Windows authentication is strongly recommended. To use SQL authentication, specify the credentials which will be used to connect to the database.

Database Server
tsinfotech

Database Name
WSS_Content_c849e2ca42baa42bca5acb

Database authentication
☑ Windows authentication (recommended)
☐ SQL authentication
   Account

   Password

Failover Server
You can choose to associate a database with a specific failover server that is used in conjunction with SQL Server database mirroring.

Failover Database Server

Service Application Connections
Choose the service applications that this Web application will be connected to. A Web application can be connected to the default set of service applications or to a custom set of service applications. You can change the set of service applications that a Web application is connected to at any time by using the Configure service application associations page in Central Administration.

Edit the following group of connections: default ▼
There are no items to show in this view.

Customer Experience Improvement Program
Collect web site analytics about web pages and site web applications. Please note that Administrators goal for before running this for web applications available over the public Internet.

Enable Customer Experience Improvement Program
☐ Yes
☑ No

Warning: In order for Quick Start Experience Improvement Program (CEIP) to collect data, both CEIP web browser CEIP on the farm level should be enabled.

OK   Cancel

3. If you are creating a web application using a browser, it will take a lot of time and you might get the *Request Timeout* error also. Alternatively, you can create a web application using PowerShell in SharePoint 2019.

Creating an application using Microsoft PowerShell

Below is the PowerShell script to create a web application in SharePoint 2019 (port no. 80). You can use PowerShell ISE or Visual Studio code to create, debug and test a PowerShell script:

```
Add-PsSnapin "Microsoft.SharePoint.PowerShell" -EA 0
$AppPoolAccount = "TSInfo\Padmini"
$ApplicationPoolName ="SharePoint 2019 App Pool"
$Description = "SharePoint 2019 Web Application"
New-SPWebApplication -ApplicationPool $ApplicationPoolName `
        -ApplicationPoolAccount (Get-SPManagedAccount $AppPoolAccount) `
        -Name $Description `
        -AuthenticationProvider (New-SPAuthenticationProvider
    -UseWindowsIntegratedAuthentication) `
        -Port 80
```

You can also create the web application using PowerShell cmdlets in SharePoint 2019 on other ports. The code is as follows:

```
Add-PsSnapin "Microsoft.SharePoint.PowerShell" -EA 0
 $AppPoolAccount = "TSInfo\Padmini"
$ApplicationPoolName ="SharePoint 2019 App Pool"
$Description = "SharePoint2019-29029"
New-SPWebApplication -ApplicationPool $ApplicationPoolName `
        -ApplicationPoolAccount (Get-SPManagedAccount $AppPoolAccount) `
        -Name $Description `
        -AuthenticationProvider (New-SPAuthenticationProvider
    -UseWindowsIntegratedAuthentication) `
        -Port 29029
```

If you miss the symbol (`) in the preceding code, then the code will not run. It will give you an error.

Once you run the PowerShell code, it will create the following web application in SharePoint 2019:

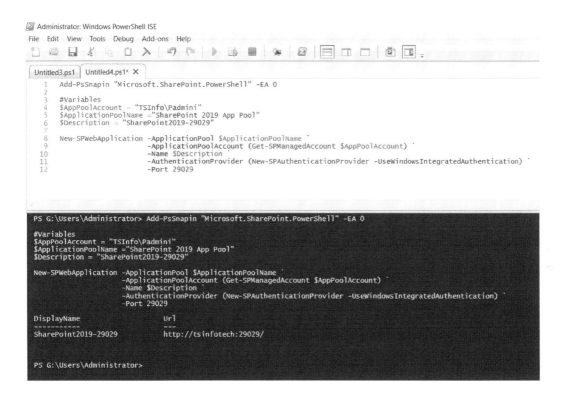

View all the web applications

To check all the web applications in SharePoint 2019, open SharePoint 2019 central administration and go to **Application Management** | **Manage Web Applications** as shown in the following screenshot:

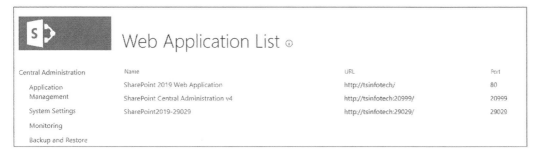

Create a site collection in SharePoint Online

Once you create a web application, you can create a site collection in SharePoint 2019.

Let us learn how to create a modern team site collection in SharePoint 2019.

To create a SharePoint 2019 site collection, follow the given steps:

1. Open your **SharePoint Central Administration**.

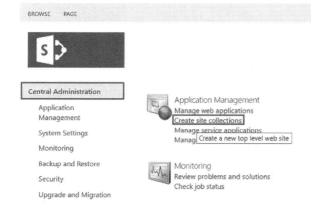

2. Click on **Create site collections** under the **Application Management** option.

3. **Create Site Collection**: In this step, you need to enter some field values to create a site collection as shown in the following screenshot. The field values are as follows:

   • **Web Application**: Select a web application to create a new site collection. You can also change the web application by using drop-down menu.

   • **Title and Description**: Enter a title and description for your new site. The title will be displayed on each page of the site.

   • **Web Site Address**: Choose to create a site at a specific path or specify the URL name and the URL path to create a new site.

   • **Template Selection**: There are four categories in this section and each category has different types of templates such as **Collaboration**, **Enterprise**, **Publishing**, and **Custom.**

Create Site Collection ⓘ

OK   Cancel

Web Application

Select a web application.

Web Application: http://tsinfotech:29029/ ▾

To create a new web application go to **New Web Application** page.

Title and Description

Type a title and description for your new site. The title will be displayed on each page in the site.

Title:

Marketing

Description:

This field is used for marketing purpose.

Web Site Address

Specify the URL name and URL path to create a new site, or choose to create a site at a specific path.

URL:

http://tsinfotech:29029 /sites/ ▾ Marketing

To add a new URL Path go to the **Define Managed Paths** page.

4. To create a modern team site, choose the **Team site** template. If you want to create a classic team site, then choose **Team site (classic experience).** You need to fill the following field values:

- **Primary Site Collection Administrator**: Specify the administrator for this site collection. Here, only one user login can be provided. Security groups are not supported.

- **Secondary Site Collection Administrator**: Specify the administrator for the Secondary site collection which is optional. Similarly, security groups are not supported.

- **Quota Template**: Select a quota template to limit resources used for this site collection. It has predefined values.

5. After filling all the field values, click on the **OK** button to create your new site collection as shown in the following screenshot:

Template Selection

Select a template:

Collaboration   Enterprise   Publishing   Custom

Team site
Team site (classic experience)
Blog
Developer Site
Project Site
Community Site

A site with no connection to an Office 365 Group.

Primary Site Collection Administrator

Specify the administrator for this site collection. Only one user login can be provided; security groups are not supported.

User name:

preeti sahu

Secondary Site Collection Administrator

Optionally specify a secondary site collection administrator. Only one user login can be provided; security groups are not supported.

User name:

preeti sahu

Quota Template

Select a predefined quota template to limit resources used for this site collection.

To add a new quota template, go to the Manage Quota Templates page.

Select a quota template:

No Quota ▼

Storage limit:

Number of invited users:

OK   Cancel

6.   After a while, you can see your new site or the top-level site will be successfully created as shown here:

Central Administration · Application Management · Top-Level Site Successfully Created

The new top-level site was created successfully with the specified URL. If you have permission to view the Web site, you can do so in a new browser window by clicking the URL. To return to SharePoint Central Administration, click **OK**.

http://tsinfotech:29029/sites/Marketing

OK

Modern SharePoint Online team site versus SharePoint 2019 team site

In this section, we will see the difference between the features available in the modern SharePoint Online team site and features missing in the SharePoint 2019 team site.

The modern SharePoint Online team site home page

There are a few differences between modern SharePoint Online team sites and SharePoint 2019 team sites which are discussed in the following sections.

The following screenshot shows how the modern SharePoint team site home page looks like. On the modern team site home page, there are four types of web parts as follows:

- **News**
- **Quick links**
- **Activity**
- **Documents**

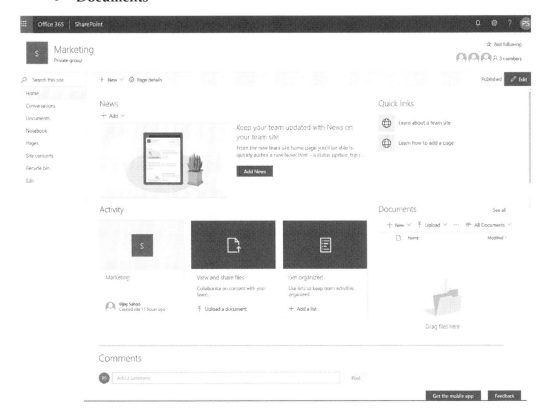

The SharePoint 2019 team site home page

The following screenshot shows how the team site home page looks like in SharePoint 2019. This home page is totally different from the SharePoint Online modern home page. There are only two web parts present in this home page which are as follows:

- **News**
- **Activity**

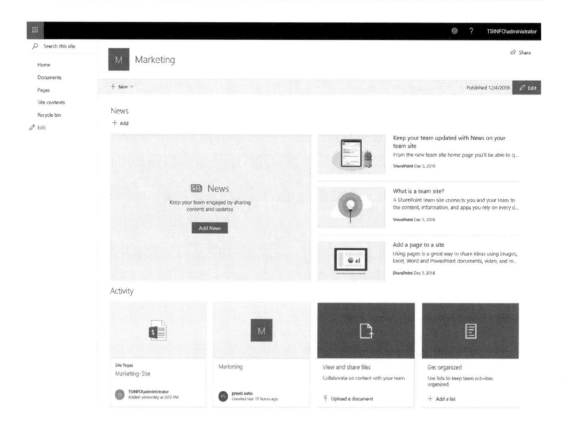

Difference between the SharePoint 2019 site and modern SharePoint Online site features

1. **Left navigation**: Left navigation helps to navigate from one page to another page by clicking just once on the link. In a SharePoint 2019 site, there are five left navigation options where as in the SharePoint Online site, there are seven left navigation options. You can view the difference in the following screenshot:

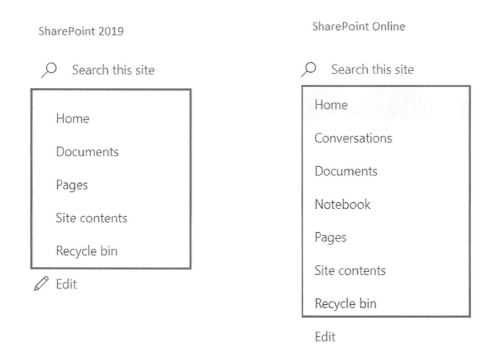

2. **Command bar**: Another difference is the command bar which is present at the top of the page. In SharePoint 2019, there is only one option in the command bar, that is, **+New**. But in the SharePoint Online command bar, there are two options: **+New** and **Page details** as shown in the following screenshot:

3. **+New command bar options**: When you go to the **+New** command bar of the SharePoint 2019 team site, you can see five options such as **List**, **Document library**, **Page,** etc. But in SharePoint Online, there are two more different options: **News link** and **Plan**. You can view the difference in the following screenshot:

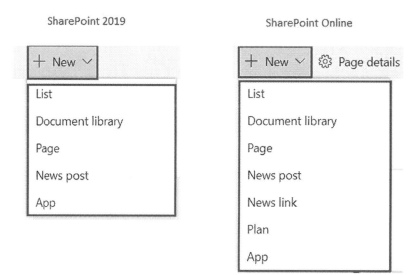

4. In SharePoint 2019, you can clearly see that there is a new option **Share** at the top of the site page. This means you can easily share this site to another user by using this option. But in SharePoint Online, there is no share option at the top of the page. Instead of the **Share** option, it shows the total number of members in the team site. When you hover your mouse over each member icon, it will show you the details of each member.

5. Another difference is that you can see a **Published** option with the published date in SharePoint 2019. But in SharePoint Online, you can see the **Published** option without any date as shown in the following screenshot:

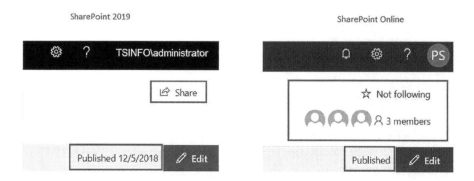

6. **Comments section**: There is no comments section on the SharePoint 2019 team site home page whereas SharePoint Online has a comments section as shown here:

Difference between SharePoint 2019 team site lists and SharePoint Online team site lists

The only one difference between SharePoint 2019 lists and SharePoint Online lists is the command bar options. If you see the difference between both the lists, you can see that there are **Flow** and **PowerApps** options available in the SharePoint Online list. But in the SharePoint 2019 list, the **Flow** and **PowerApps** options are missing in the command bar because of SharePoint On-Premises:

Difference between the SharePoint 2019 team site library and the SharePoint Online team site library

The only one difference between the SharePoint 2019 team site library and the SharePoint Online team site library is the command bar options. If you see the difference between both the libraries, you can see that there is a **Flow** option available in the SharePoint Online team site library. But in the SharePoint 2019 team site library, the **Flow** option is missing in the command bar because of SharePoint On-Premises:

Web parts available in the SharePoint 2019 team site

- Text
- Image
- File viewer
- Embed
- Highlighted
- List
- Divider
- Image gallery
- Spacer
- Stream (preview)
- Document library
- Hero
- Highlighted content
- List
- Quick links
- Events
- News
- People
- Yammer
- Quick chart
- Site activity

Web parts not available in the SharePoint 2019 team site

- Link
- Bing Maps
- Kindle Instant Preview
- Office 365 video
- Weather
- YouTube
- Page properties
- Recent documents
- Sites
- Group calendar
- Microsoft Forms
- Twitter (preview)
- Planner
- Power BI
- Asana
- Bitbucket
- Bitbucket Server
- Facebook Pages
- GitHub
- GitHub Enterprise
- Google Analytics
- Incoming Webhooks
- JIRA
- Microsoft PowerApps (preview)

- Office 365 Connectors

- RSS

- Salesforce

- Stack Overflow

- Trello

- UserVoice

- Wunderlist

- Code Snippet

SharePoint 2019 Modern UI

The above SharePoint 2019 modern UI portal consists of five web parts. To know more about this portal, let us take a look at the following points:

- **Hero**: The first section shows the **Hero** web part. By using this hero web part, you can display up to five items with compelling images, texts and links to draw attention to each item. If you want to show five items at a time with some text, images and links, then you can easily use this web part.

- **News**: The **News** web part helps to add some latest news of an organization. By using this web part, you can update with yourself. This web part is used in second section of the portal given below.

- **Embed**: The third section shows the **Embed** web part which helps to display any image or video. Once you put any embed code or URL, it will help you to add the video or image in that web part.

- **Events**: When you add an event to the site page, the **Events** web part helps to show the event here where your readers can see it. So the fourth section shows the **Event** web part. By using this web part, you can add a number of upcoming events of your organization.

- **People**: The **People** web part displays the profile information of a selected group of people by adding their custom links and description of each person. This is shown in the fifth section in the portal.

+ New ∨   Published 12/6/2018 ✏ Edit

News

+ Add

How we manage market growth?
We have been expanding rapidly to the new markets across the world. This is great but how do we manag...
TSINFO\administrator 2 hours ago

Monthly Update Adventure Travel
December has been an excellent month for Adventure Travel program. We are going to launch a new offerin...
TSINFO\administrator 2 hours ago

Adventure Travel Opportunity
It has an enormous landscape and wildlife diversity. There is a tremendous opportunity to expand our Ad...
TSINFO\administrator 2 hours ago

Make your customer dream come true!
Our program is based on hard work that each team member puts in helping our customers realization.
TSINFO\administrator 3 hours ago

Trip Overviews

Travel in Cappadocia

Travel in Himalayan

Travel in South Italy

Upcoming Events

+ Add event   See all

DEC 15	DEC 17	DEC 20	DEC 22
Upcoming itinerary seminar	Adventure travel AMA	Destination deep dive-ICELAND	Coffee break series-Italy
Sat, Dec 15, 4:00 PM bangalore	Mon, Dec 17, 3:00 PM	Thu, Dec 20, 10:30 AM	Sat, Dec 22, 4:00 PM
🗓 Add to my calendar	🗓 Add to my calendar	🗓 Add to my calendar	🗓 Add to my calendar

Your Adventure Travel Team

 preeti sahu   padmini p   BD bibhu data

Summery

In this chapter we discussed, modern experience in SharePoint server 2019. Few new features of SharePoint server 2019, how to create web application using SharePoint server 2019 central administration as well as using PowerShell.

We also discussed how to create a modern team site collection in SharePoint server 2019. Difference between the SharePoint 2019 site and modern SharePoint Online site features etc.

In the next chapter we will discuss on SharePoint 2019 communication site.

CHAPTER 10

SharePoint 2019 Communication Site

Microsoft released communication site templates in SharePoint Online and in SharePoint Server 2019. A SharePoint communication site is a great place to share information with others. You can share news, reports, statuses, and other information in a visually appealing format. In this chapter, we will discuss the following topics:

- Difference between the creation of a SharePoint 2019 communication site and SharePoint Online communication site

- Difference between a SharePoint 2019 communication site home page and SharePoint Online communication site

- Availability and non-availability between a SharePoint 2019 communication site and modern SharePoint Online communication site

- Difference between a SharePoint 2019 communication site list and SharePoint Online communication site list

- Difference between a SharePoint 2019 communication site library and SharePoint Online communication site library

- Availability and non- availability of SharePoint 2019 communication site web parts

SharePoint 2019 communication sites versus SharePoint Online communication sites

Now, let us see a few differences between SharePoint 2019 communication sites and SharePoint Online communication sites. Before that, let us see how to create a communication site in SharePoint 2019 and SharePoint Online.

Create a SharePoint 2019 communication site

Once you create a web application, you can create a site collection in SharePoint 2019.

Let us see how to create a modern communication site collection in SharePoint 2019.

To create a SharePoint 2019 communication site collection, follow the given steps:

1. Open your **SharePoint Central Administration**.

2. Click on **Create Site Collection** under the **Application Management** tab.

3. You need to create a site collection in the **Create Site Collection** window. In this step, you need to enter some field values to create a site collection as shown in the following screenshot. The field values are as follows:

    *   **Web Application**: Select a web application to create a new site collection. You can also change the web application by using the drop-down menu.

    *   **Title and Description**: Enter a title and description for your new communication site. The title will be displayed on each page of the site.

    *   **Web Site Address**: Specify the URL name and URL path to create a new site or choose to create a site at a specific path.

    *   **Template Selection**: There are four categories and each category has different types of templates as follows:

    *   **Collaboration**

    *   **Enterprise**

    *   **Publishing**

    *   **Custom**

To create a modern communication site, choose the **Publishing** category and then click on the **Communication Site** template. You need to fill the field values for the following:

- **Primary Site Collection Administrator**: Specify the administrator for the site collection. Here, only one user login can be provided. This field does not support security groups.

- **Secondary Site Collection Administrator**: Specify an administrator for the secondary site collection which is optional. Similarly, this field does not support any security groups.

- **Quota Template**: Select a quota template to limit resources used for this site collection. It has predefined values.

After filling all the field values, click on the **OK** button to create your new communication site collection as shown in the following screenshot:

Create Site Collection ⓘ

| | | OK | Cancel |

Web Application
Select a web application.

To create a new web application go to New Web Application page.

Web Application: http://tsinfotech:29029/ ▾

Title and Description
Type a title and description for your new site. The title will be displayed on each page in the site.

Title:
Support

Description:
This Site is used for Support purpose.

Web Site Address
Specify the URL name and URL path to create a new site, or choose to create a site at a specific path.

To add a new URL Path go to the Define Managed Paths page.

URL:
http://tsinfotech:29029 /sites/ ▾ Support

Template Selection

Select a template:

Collaboration   Enterprise   **Publishing**   Custom

Publishing Portal
Enterprise Wiki
Product Catalog
Communication site

Publish dynamic, beautiful content to people in your organization to keep them informed and engaged on topics, events, or projects.

Primary Site Collection Administrator
Specify the administrator for this site collection. Only one user login can be provided; security groups are not supported.

User name:
TSINFO\administrator

Secondary Site Collection Administrator
Optionally specify a secondary site collection administrator. Only one user login can be provided; security groups are not supported.

User name:
TSINFO\administrator

Quota Template
Select a predefined quota template to limit resources used for this site collection.

To add a new quota template, go to the Manage Quota Templates page.

Select a quota template:
No Quota ▾

Storage limit:
Number of invited users:

| | | OK | Cancel |

After a while, you can see your new communication site or the top-level site will be successfully created as shown in the following screenshot:

Central Administration · Application Management · Top-Level Site Successfully Created

The new top-level site was created successfully with the specified URL. If you have permission to view the Web site, you can do so in a new browser window by clicking the URL. To return to SharePoint Central Administration, click **OK** .

http://tsinfotech:29029/sites/Support

OK

Create a SharePoint Online communication site

Let us see how to create a modern communication site collection in SharePoint Online.

To create a SharePoint Online communication site collection, follow the given steps:

1. Open your **SharePoint Admin Center**.

2. Click on **Check out the new SharePoint admin center** and then click on the **Try it now** option.

3. Click on **Active Sites** under the **Sites** option which is present in the left navigation.

4. Click on **+ Create** to create a communication site.

5. Choose the **Communication Site** template as shown in following screenshot.

If you want to create a team site or any other site, you can click on the **Team site** window. As you need to create a new communication site, you need to choose **Communication site**.

Create a site

Choose the type of site you'd like to create.

Team site

Share documents, have conversations with your team, keep track of events, manage tasks, and more with a site connected to an Office 365 group.

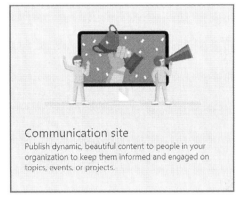

Communication site

Publish dynamic, beautiful content to people in your organization to keep them informed and engaged on topics, events, or projects.

Other options

Create a new team site without an Office 365 group, or a Document center, Enterprise wiki, Publishing portal, or Project Web App site.

6. Once you select **Communication Site**, it will ask you to select a design from the drop-down menu. Choose your communication site design as per your requirement. In this step, you need to enter some field values to create a site collection as shown in the following screenshot. The field values are as follows:

    - **Site name**: Enter a name which you want to give for your communication site.

    - **Site address**: Choose to create a site at a specific path or specify the URL name and URL path.

    - **Site owner**: Specify the owner username for the communication site.

    - **Select a language**: Select the default site language for your site which you cannot change later.

    - **Time zone**: Select a specific time zone for your site.

    - **Site description**: Enter a description for your new communication site.

    - **Storage limit**: Enter a storage limit for the resources used for this site collection.

7. After filling all the field values, click on the **Finish** button to create your new communication site collection as shown in the following screenshot:

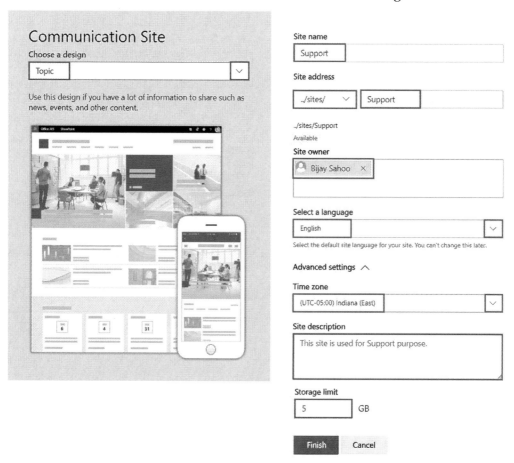

8. When you click on the **Finish** button, the communication site will be created and will be stored in **Active Sites**. This means your communication site is successfully created in SharePoint Online as shown in the following screenshot:

Difference between a SharePoint 2019 communication site home page and a SharePoint Online communication site home page

There are a few differences between modern SharePoint Online communication sites and SharePoint 2019 communication sites which are discussed in the following sections.

The SharePoint 2019 communication site home page

The following screenshot shows how the communication site home page looks like in SharePoint 2019. This home page looks very similar to the SharePoint Online modern communication site home page. The four web parts on this home page are as follows:

- **Hero**
- **News**
- **Events**
- **Highlighted content**

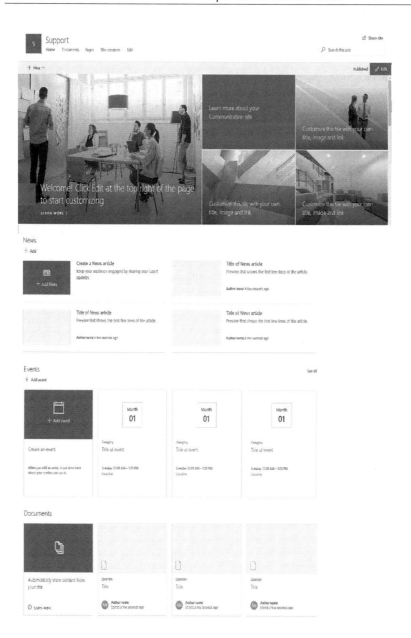

The SharePoint Online communication site home page

The following screenshot shows how the modern SharePoint online communication site home page looks like. Similarly, in the modern SharePoint Online communication site home page, there are four types of web parts as given here:

- **Hero**
- **News**
- **Events**

Highlighted content

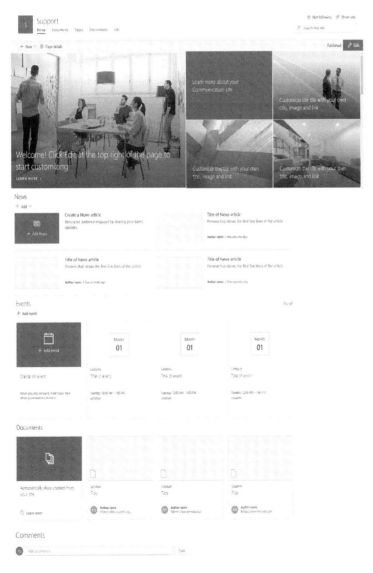

Create the header and footer navigation in a SharePoint online communication site

Header navigation:

To create the header navigation link, go to **Settings (gear)** icon and then click on **Change the Look**.

In the **Change the look** dialogue box, click on the **Navigation** option as shown below:

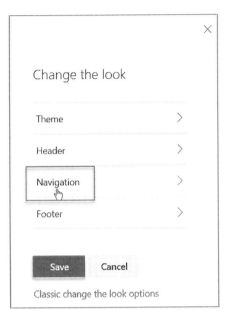

When you click on **Navigation**, it will display the following two types of the menu style:

- Megamenu
- Cascading

Select any one menu style, click on **Apply**, and then close the navigation.

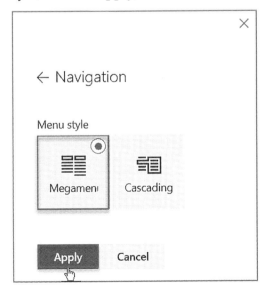

Now, go to the **Edit** link which is present on the top link bar of the communication site page.

After clicking on the **Edit** link, a dialogue box will appear on the left-hand side of the page where you can add the navigation links for the header.

In this dialogue box, place the cursor at any place and then click on the + symbol. Once you click on the + symbol, an **Add a link** box will appear where you need to fill the following fields:

- Choose an option: In this field, there are two types of options:

- **URL**: If you want to make the navigation link option as the URL, then choose this one.

- **Header**: If you want to make the navigation link option as the Header, then choose this one.

In this following example, I have chosen the option as **Header** from the drop-down menu.

- **Address**: Provide the URL address of the navigation link which you want to make as the footer. In this example, I have selected the option as the Header, so I did not provide any address over here.

- **Display name**: Enter a name for the navigation link.

After filling all the field values, click on **OK** as shown in the following screenshot:

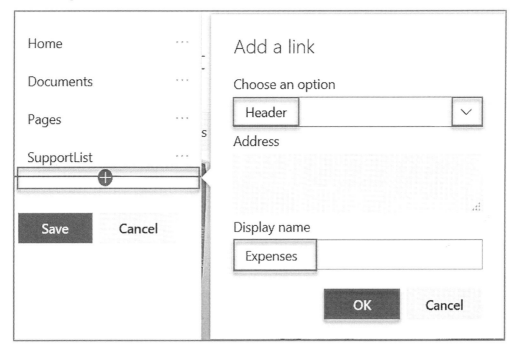

To make the sub link of the header, click on the **…** symbol and then click on **Make sub link** as shown in the following screenshot:

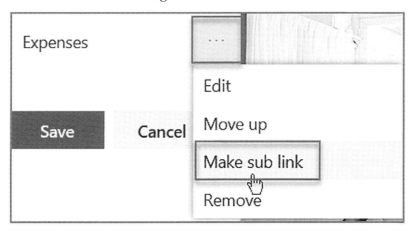

In the same way, I have created another link where I chose the option **URL** and fill the remaining filed values.

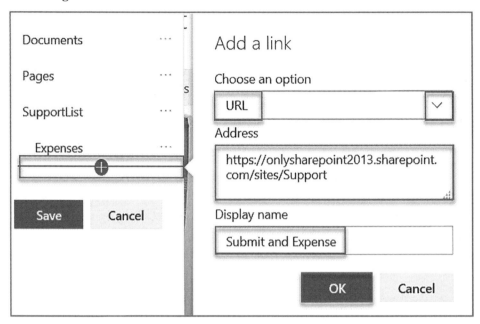

Similarly, I have created another navigation where the option is **Header** and I have given the display name as **Onboarding**.

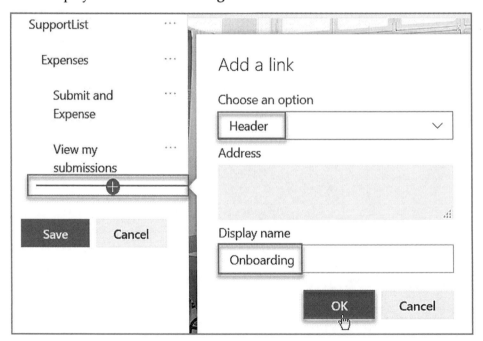

I made this **Onboarding** navigation to promote sub links as shown below:

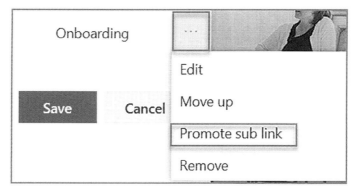

Under the **Onboarding** header, I have created a sub link named **Key Documents** with the **URL** option.

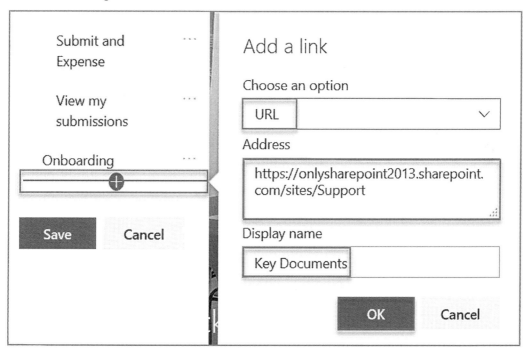

Now, make this **Key Documents** as the sub link by using the **Make sub link** option.

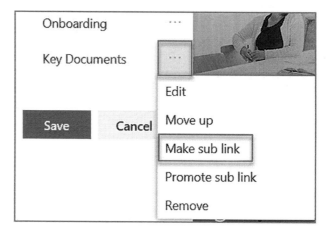

In the same way, I have created another navigation link named **Key Contacts**. You can see all the header navigation links in the following screenshot. Just click on **Save**.

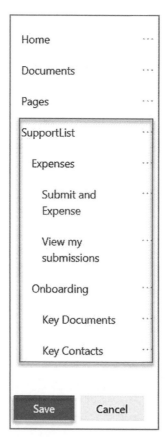

Once it is done, click on **SupportList**. You can see all the promoted sub links and sub links in the following screenshot. Since the menu style is **Megamenu**, the navigation style looks like the menu type.

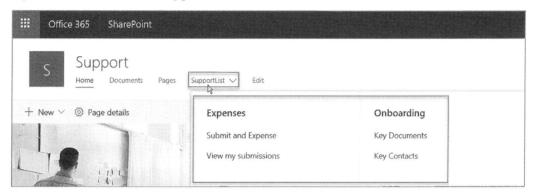

If you want to change the navigation menu style, then go to **Navigation** | **Cascading** | **Apply**.

When you click on **SupportList**, all the promoted sub links and sub links will be displayed as shown in the following screenshot:

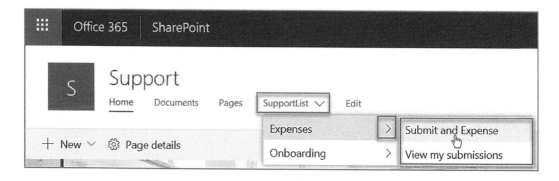

Footer navigation

1. Go to the **Settings (gear)** icon and then click on **Change the look**.

2. In the **Change the look** dialogue box, click on the **Footer** option as shown below:

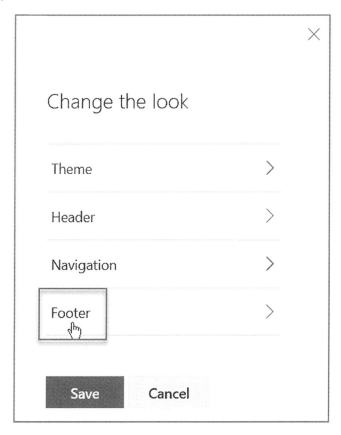

3. When the **Footer** page opens, the page will look as shown in the following screenshot. The footer section has the following fields:

    *   **Footer visibility**: When this is enabled, the footer part will be visible or else this will not be visible.

    *   **Logo**: Logo helps you to put an image in the footer section. If you want to put an image, click on **Upload**, choose your logo from your PC and then save it.

    *   **Footer name visibility**: When this is enabled, the footer name will visible or else this will not be visible.

    *   **Footer name**: You need to provide a name for the footer section.

- **Edit footer navigation links**: You can edit or enter your navigation links by using this option.

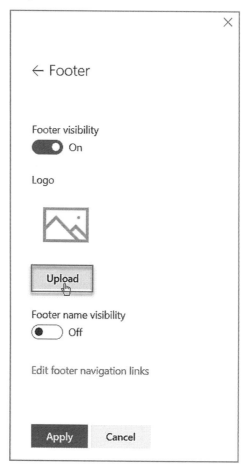

4. When you upload the footer image, it will look as shown in the following screenshot. If you want to change or delete the image, you can use the **Change** and **Remove** options.

5. To create footer navigation links, just click on **Edit footer navigation links**.

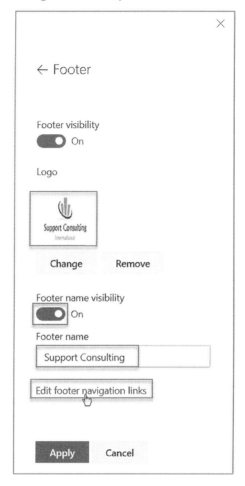

6. After clicking on **Edit footer navigation links**, a dialogue box will appear on the left-hand side of the page where you can add the navigation links.

7. In this dialogue box, put the cursor at any place and then click on the **+** symbol. When you click on the **+** symbol, an **Add a link** box will appear on the screen where you need to fill the following fields:

8. Choose an option: In this field, there are two types of options:

    - **URL**: If you want to make the navigation link option as the URL, then choose this one.

    - **Header**: If you want to make the navigation link option as the Header, then choose this one.

In the following example, I have chosen the option **URL** from the drop-down menu.

- **Address**: Provide the URL address of the navigation link which you want to make as the footer.

- **Display name**: Enter a name for the navigation link.

After filling all the field values, click on **OK** as shown in the following screenshot:

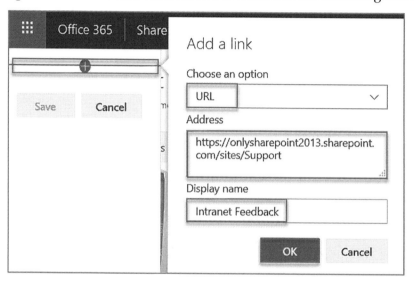

9. In the same way, I have created another navigation named **Training Center** and clicked on **OK**.

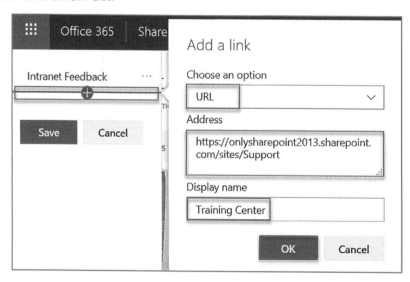

10. After creating four navigation links, the page will look as shown in the following screenshot. Then, click on **Save**.

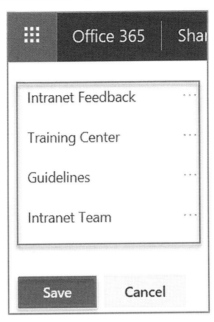

11. Now, go to the footer part of the page (below Comments). Here, you can see the footer logo with the footer name and all navigation links which you have created.

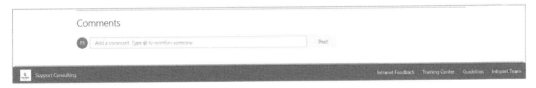

Availability and non-availability between SharePoint 2019 communication sites and modern SharePoint Online communication sites

In this section we will see, what are the things which as available and not available in SharePoint server 2019 communication site compare to SharePoint Online communication sites?

Note: The features that I am showing here is what is presented at the time of writing this book, later it may change.

1. **No Left Navigation**: Left navigation helps to navigate from one page to another page by clicking once on the link. In the SharePoint2019 site and the SharePoint Online site, there is no left navigation. Instead of left navigation, there is a top navigation in both the sites.

2. In the SharePoint Online communication site, you can clearly see that there is an option named **Not following** at the top of the site page but it is not available in the SharePoint 2019 communication site:

3. **Command bar**: Another difference between the two is the command bar which is present at the top of the page. In SharePoint 2019, there is only one option in the command bar, that is, **+New**. But in the SharePoint Online command bar, there are two options: **+New** and **Page details** which is shown in the following screenshot:

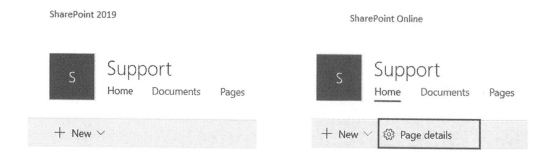

4. **+New** command bar options: Once you go to the **+New** command bar of the SharePoint 2019 communication site, you will see five options such as **List**, **Document library**, **Page**, **News post** and **App**. But in SharePoint Online, there are two more different options: **News link** and **Plan**. You can view the differences in the following screenshot:

SharePoint 2019

SharePoint Online

5. **Comments**: There is no comments section on the SharePoint 2019 communication site home page whereas the SharePoint Online communication site has a comments section as shown here:

SharePoint Online

6. **Settings**: If you go to the **Settings** option of the SharePoint 2019, you can view only six options where as in SharePoint Online, you can see seven options. The extra option is **Site usage** which is not available in SharePoint 2019 as shown here:

SharePoint 2019

SharePoint Online

Difference between a SharePoint 2019 communication site list and SharePoint Online communication site list

The only difference between a SharePoint 2019 communication site list and SharePoint Online communication site list is the **Command Bar** options. If you see the difference between both the lists, you can see that there are **Flow** and **PowerApps** options available in the SharePoint Online list. But in the SharePoint 2019 list, there are no **Flow** and **PowerApps** options available in the command bar because of SharePoint On-Premises:

Difference between a SharePoint 2019 communication site library and SharePoint Online communication site library

The only difference between a SharePoint 2019 communication site library and SharePoint Online communication site library is the **Command Bar** options. If you see the difference between both the libraries, you can see that there is a **Flow** option available in the SharePoint Online library. But in the SharePoint 2019 Library, there is no **Flow** option in the command bar because of SharePoint On-Premises:

Web Parts available in a SharePoint 2019 Communication Site

- Text
- Image
- File viewer
- Embed
- Highlighted
- List
- Divider
- Image gallery
- Spacer
- Stream (preview)
- Document library
- Hero
- Highlighted content
- List

- Quick links
- Events
- News
- People
- Yammer
- Quick chart
- Site activity

Web parts not available in SharePoint 2019 communication site

- Link
- Bing Maps
- Kindle Instant Preview
- Office 365 video
- Weather
- YouTube
- Page properties
- Recent documents
- Sites
- Group calendar
- Microsoft Forms
- Twitter (preview)
- Planner
- Power BI
- Asana
- Bitbucket
- Bitbucket Server
- Facebook Pages
- GitHub
- GitHub Enterprise

- Google Analytics
- Incoming Webhooks
- JIRA
- Microsoft PowerApps (preview)
- Office 365 Connectors
- RSS
- Salesforce
- Stack Overflow
- Trello
- UserVoice
- Wunderlist
- Code Snippet

Summary

In this chapter, we learned about SharePoint Online communication sites, how to create a communication site in SharePoint Online and SharePoint Server 2019. We also took a look at how SharePoint 2019 communication sites and SharePoint Online communication look like. We also learned about various web parts in SharePoint Online and the SharePoint Server 2019 communication site.

In the next chapter we will discuss, what's not possible in SharePoint Online modern experience.

CHAPTER 11

SharePoint Online Modern Experience – What's not possible?

Although the SharePoint Online modern experience has remarkable features which greatly increases its usability and acceptability, there are a few limitations. We will discuss these limitations in this chapter.

Customizations unsupported in modern team sites

The following things are still not supported in modern team sites. And if your organization requires these things, then think before taking a decision to move to new modern team sites:

- Custom page layouts or master pages are not supported in modern team sites. Neither can you use classic *seattle.master* or *oslo.master* master pages in modern team sites.

- You cannot embed a custom JavaScript or custom actions in modern team sites. You can easily embed a custom JavaScript using the Script Editor in classic team sites. These things can be done using the SharePoint framework. You can do lots of client side development using Microsoft framework development model. Scripting capabilities are not available in modern team sites.

- Sandboxed solutions are not supported in modern team sites.

- You cannot open a SharePoint Online modern team site using SharePoint Designer 2013.

- Some of the popular web parts are not available for end users in modern team sites.

- *Save Site as a Template* is not possible in a modern SharePoint site.

- You cannot add *Task List* and *Issue tracking* list directly to a modern site page as a web part. Instead of taking the *Task List* and *Issue tracking* list, recreate the list as a *Custom List*. Then, you can add these two lists to your list web part.

Customization is impossible in a modern document library

Here are a few customizations that are NOT possible, so we need to understand according to our requirement:

- JSLink-based field or view customizations are not possible in the SharePoint Online modern document library.

- Custom CSS via **AlternateCSSUrl** web property is not possible. **JSLink** customization was quite popular among developers.

- Most of the times we embed a custom JavaScript using the Script Editor inside the page, but in the modern document library, this kind of customization is not possible.

- A custom JavaScript embedded via the user custom actions are not supported.

- Custom master pages, **Minimal Download Strategy** (**MDS**) and SharePoint Server Publishing are not supported.

- InfoPath has a huge impact in the new modern document library. Customization using InfoPath is not supported.

- So, if you have any library which is customized using InfoPath, you cannot move it as it is.

- Microsoft has released a new development model to work with SharePoint Online modern sites or SharePoint server 2019 modern sites known as the SharePoint Framework.

The SharePoint Framework development is outside the scope of this book. But you can watch a video and tutorial on how you can set up the SharePoint framework development environment with a hello word development environment.

Video: https://www.youtube.com/watch?v=-8-aIBmjVPo

Tutorial: https://www.sharepointsky.com/sharepoint-framework-development/

Summary

In this book, we learned about SharePoint Online modern experiences or the modern UI, how to work with modern team sites, communication sites, modern site pages, modern lists and document libraries.

We also saw how to design portals using various out-of-the-box web parts in SharePoint Online Office 365.

We also learned how to create modern team sites in SharePoint server 2019, the latest version of SharePoint On-Premises.

We looked at the customizations which are not possible in SharePoint Online modern team sites as well as customizations that are impossible in SharePoint Online modern document libraries.

Index

A

ActiveX, 35
Active Directory 4
Add an app option
  using, 4-8
AlternateCSSUrl web property, 1
auto-pagination, 50

B

Bing maps web part, 12

C

Classic SharePoint Online Experience
  about, 1-3
  lifespan, 6-8
classic SharePoint Team, 1
classic team site
  creating, in Classic
      Admin Center, 18, 19
  home page look, changing, 21-23
cloud solution 2

column
  customizing, JSON used, 63
  formatting, JSON used, 63

D

Document Library, 16
divider web part, 14
document details pane, 16
document library (preview)
      web part, 15, 16
document management, features
  about 4
  Advanced Threat
  Protection (ATP) 5
  Data Loss Prevention (DLP) 4
  version, updation 5
  download as Zip option, 19

E

Enterprise Social Network (ESN), 82
embed web part, 9, 10
events web part, 16-19

F

file viewer web part, 7, 8
footer navigation
  about, 21-28
  creating, in SharePoint Online com-
    munication site, 11-20

G

GitHub web part, 20-23
Groups, 2
Groups, fields
  description, 2
  Group email address, 2
  Group name, 2
  group-related
  notifications, language, 2
  privacy, 2

H

header navigation
creating, in SharePoint Online com-
    munication site, 11-20
hero web part, 23-28
highlighted content web part, 11
hub site
  advantages, in SharePoint
    Online, 5
  features, in SharePoint Online, 5
  in SharePoint Online, 4

I

Image gallery web part, layouts
  Brick layout, 34
Internet Information Services (IIS), 4
image gallery web part, 29-33
image gallery web part, layouts
  Carousel layout, 33
  Tiles layout, 33

image web part, 5, 6

J

JIRA connector web part, 34, 35
JSLink customization, 1

L

link web part, 8, 9
list (preview) web part, 36

M

Microsoft Cloud Service 2
Microsoft Flow
  reference link, 27
Microsoft Forms
  about, 42-44
  copy option, 44
  delete option, 44
  move down option, 44
  move up option, 44
Microsoft Forms, properties
  about, 45-49
  preview, 45
  share, 47
  theme, 46
Microsoft PowerShell
  used, for creating web application, 6
Minimal Download Strategy (MDS), 1
Modern SharePoint
  left navigation, removing, 37-39
Modern SharePoint
    Online Experience
  about, 5, 6
  document library, 12-14
  enabling, at tenant l
    evel in Office 365, 9-12
  list library, 12-14
  supported browsers, 6

switching, to Modern
  UI Experience, 15, 16
modern document library
  customizing, 1
modern SharePoint Online
    site features
    versus SharePoint 2019
    site features, 13-16
modern SharePoint Online
    document library
  Add an app option, used, 4-7
  Alert Me notification, 35
  Bulk Edit properties, 31, 32
  column width, changing, 13
  column, creating, 9-13
  copy link option, 22, 23
  creating, 2
  document details pane, 16, 17
  document shared, stopping, 23-25
  document, sharing, 20, 21
  document, uploading, 13, 14
  documents, selecting
    in .zip format, 19, 20
  ECB Menu, opening, 50, 51
  Edit New menu, 53-55
  Edit New menu option, 56-59
  edit view column, 47-49
  Export to Excel feature, 35
  features, 8
  file attention, 51-53
  Filter by Column, 42, 43
  Group by Column, 44
  Library Column, ordering
    as ascending, 36
  Library Column, ordering
    as descending, 36
  library settings page, accessing, 8
  mandatory field validation
    notification, 36-41
  Microsoft Flow, creating, 33
  outlook option, 22, 23

  pin to top option, 33, 34
  Quick edit option, 14, 15
  save view as, 45-47
  selected document, copying from
    one site to another site, 30, 31
  selected document, moving from
    one site to another site, 26-29
  Site contents option, used, 2-4
  templates, adding, 60-62
modern SharePoint Online library
  column customizing, JSON used, 63
  column formatting, JSON used, 63
  item, formatting, 64-67
modern SharePoint Online list
  about, 1, 2
  Action Button, adding to field, 68-72
  Add an app option, used, 5-8
  alerts setting up, alert me
    future used, 31
  auto-pagination, 50
  background, changing
    of column, 82-84
  Button, creating to
    launch flow, 72-75
  clickable actions, creating
    into Hyperlinks, 79-81
  column added, by
    + Symbol used, 15
  column customizing, JSON used, 63
  column formatting, JSON used, 63
  column width, changing, 17
  column, adding, 10-14
  column, dragging
    to position, 18-20
  column, dropping
    to position, 18-20
  conditional formatting, in
    choice field, 85-88
  conditional formatting, in
    text field, 85-88
  creating, 2

ECB menu, opening, 54
Excel (Google Chrome),
    exporting to, 25, 26
features, 9
Filter by, Column, 41-44
Group by option, 53
item, creating, 20, 21
item, formatting, 64-67
item, sharing, 31-33
items feature, 55-57
link, copying, 34-36
list details pane, 15, 16
list item, editing, 22-24
List Settings page, accessing, 10
mandatory field
    validation notification, 45-49
Microsoft Flow, creating, 26, 27
number column, formatting
    as data bar, 76-78
order feature, 39
outlook features, 34-36
PowerApps, 27-30
ribbon, avoiding, 9
save view feature, 50-52
Site contents option, used, 2-4
stop sharing feature, 36-38
text color, changing of column, 82-84
user details, displaying on mouse
    hover, 57-60
modern SharePoint Online team site
  home page, 11
  versus SharePoint 2019 team site, 10
modern SharePoint Site pages
  creating, 1
  creating, Site contents used, 2, 3
  left navigation bar, used, 4, 5
  page layouts, 12-15
modern SharePoint web parts, 16
modern site page
  adding, to navigation, 10, 11
  customizing, as home page, 9, 10

modern team site
  adding, from Outlook, 2-4
  creating, from SharePoint Online
      Modern Admin Center, 5-9, 11
  deleting, 40-42
modern UI portal
  document library (preview), 4
  events, 3
  hero, 3
  image, 3
  link, 3, 4
  news, 3
  people, 4
  quick chart, 3
  quick links, 3
  text, 3
  weather, 3
modern team site
  unsupported, customizing, 0

N

New Insurance page, 13, 14
New TS Corporate portal, 16
news web part
  about 37, 38
  properties, 39
news web part, layouts
  hub news, 41
  list, 40
  side-by-side, 40
  top story, 39

O

Office 365
  about 2
  overview 2
  subscription, sign up 5
Office 365, benefits
  accessing 3

Active Directory, integrating 4
  data, securing 4
  document management, features 4
  large scale organization 3
  paying 3
  responsive devices 4
  SharePoint Online, advantages 4
  zero downtime 3
Office 365 Developer Program
  reference link 7
Office 365 Enterprise E3 6
  reference link 7
Office 365 , price and features
  reference link 6
Office 365, requisites
  Office 365 Business plans 6
  Office 365 plans 5
  Office Education plans 5
  Office Home plans 5
order feature
  Newer, to Older option, 40
  Older, to Newer option, 39
  Office 365 videos, 50, 51

P

people web part, 52-57
Power BI web part, 58, 59
Private, 2
Project Management page, 11, 12
properties web part, 13
Public, 2

Q

Quick Chart web part, 59-62
Quick links web part, 63-69

S

section layout

delete section, 16
  edit section, 16
  move section, 16
  properties, 15
select site, 39
SharePoint 2019 central
      administration
  used, for creating
      web application, 4, 6
SharePoint 2019 communication
      site library
  versus SharePoint Online communi-
      cation site library, 32
SharePoint 2019 communication
      site list
  versus SharePoint Online
      communication site list, 31
SharePoint 2019 communication sites
  availability, 28-30
  creating, 2, 3
  non-availability, 28-30
  versus SharePoint Online
      communication sites, 1
  web parts, 32, 33
  web parts, avoiding, 33, 34
SharePoint 2019 communication
      sites home page
  about, 7
  versus SharePoint Online communi-
      cation site home page, 7
SharePoint 2019 modern
      UI, web parts
  Embed web part, 19
  Event web part, 20
  Hero web part, 19
  News web part, 19
  People web part, 20
SharePoint 2019 modern UI, 19
SharePoint 2019 site features
  versus modern SharePoint Online
      site features, 13-16

SharePoint 2019 team site
  versus modern SharePoint Online
      team site, 10
  web parts, 17, 18
  web parts, avoiding, 18, 19
SharePoint 2019 team site library
  versus SharePoint Online
      team site library, 17
SharePoint 2019 team site lists
  versus SharePoint Online
      team site lists, 16
SharePoint Framework (SPFx), 1
SharePoint framework
      development environment
  references, 1
SharePoint Online
  about 7
  hub site, 4
  modern site pages, 5, 6
  modern site pages tabs, 8, 9
  modern site pages, designing, 6, 7
  modern site pages, web
      parts adding, 16-19
  modern team site, 1
  modern team site, content
      page, 32-35
  modern team site, creating from
      SharePoint Online
      admin center, 11-17
  modern team site, log
      changing, 28-31
  modern team site, setting
      options, 35, 36
  organization, benefits 8
  site collection, creating, 8-10
  site information, 24-26
SharePoint Online
      communication site
  availability, 28-30
  creating, 4-7
  footer navigation, creating, 11-20

header navigation, creating, 11-20
non-availability, 28-30
versus SharePoint 2019
      communication sites, 1
SharePoint Online admin center
  reference link, 11
SharePoint Online communication
      site home page
  about, 8, 9
  versus SharePoint 2019 communica-
      tion sites home page, 7
SharePoint Online communication
      site library
  versus SharePoint 2019
      communication site library, 32
SharePoint Online communication
      site list
  versus SharePoint 2019
      communication site list, 31
SharePoint Online team site
  home page, 12
SharePoint Online team site library
  versus SharePoint 2019 team
      site library, 17
SharePoint Online team site lists
  versus SharePoint 2019 team
      site lists, 16
SharePoint Online, advantages
  highly secured 7
  Microsoft data centers 7
  quick access, to updates 7
  zero downtime 8
SharePoint Server 2019
  about, 1
  web application, 3
  web application, creating, 4
SharePoint Server 2019, features
  about, 2
  communication sites, 3
  modern libraries, 3
  modern list, 3

modern site pages, 2, 3
modern team sites, 2
modern user experiences, 2
SharePoint, 1
Single Sign-On 4
Site activity web part
  about, 70, 71
  properties, 72
site collection creating, in
    SharePoint Online, 8-10
Site contents option
  using, 2-4
Sites web part
  about, 72, 73
  properties, 74
Sites web part, layouts
  Cards layout, 74
  Filmstrip layout, 74

T

text web part
  about, 1-3
  deleting, 5
  designer properties, 2
  moving, 5
this site, 39
Tiles view
  compact list, 19
  of documents, 17, 18
Timer wcb part
  about, 84-88
  fields, 85, 86
TSInfo
  home page, 4
  software development portal com-
    pany portal, 1
  technologies, 6, 8
  training site, 9
Twitter web part
  about, 75

properties, 76-79

U

Upload feature, 13

W

Weather web part, 80
Weather web part, properties
  about, 81
  celsius, 81
  fahrenheit, 81
web application
  creating, in SharePoint
    Server 2019, 4
  creating, Microsoft
    PowerShell used, 6
  creating, SharePoint 2019 central
    administration used, 4
  in SharePoint Server 2019, 3
  viewing, 7
web configuration file
  reference link, 4
web parts
  development site, 10

Y

Yammer web part, 82

55770054R00204